SEPECAT
JAGUAR

Foulis

ISBN 0 85429 438 4

A FOULIS Aircraft Book

First Published 1984

© **Winchmore Publishing Services Ltd 1984**

Published by:
Haynes Publishing Group
Sparkford, Yeovil,
Somerset BA22 7JJ

Distributed in USA by:
Haynes Publications Inc.
861 Lawrence Drive,
Newbury Park,
California 91320, USA

Produced by:
Winchmore Publishing Services Limited,
40 Triton Square,
London NW1 3HG

Printed in Yugoslavia by Mladinska Knjiga

Chant, Christopher
    Sepecat Jaguar.—(Super profile)
    1. Jaguar (Jet attack plane)
    I. Title   II. Series
    623.74'63   UG1242.F5

    ISBN 0-85429-438-4

Contents

Further titles in this series will be published at
regular intervals. For information on new titles
please contact your bookseller or write to the
publisher.

Genesis

The origins of the SEPECAT Jaguar date back to the early 1960s, and the joint British and French project which led to the creation of the aircraft was the world's first successfuly to produce a front-line combat aircraft out of a full international collaborative programme. This was especially remarkable because the two countries involved have traditionally been mutually mistrustful of each other's intentions, and political differences had recently been sharpened in any case by French opposition to British entry into the European Economic Community. On the surface the prospect of Anglo-French co-operation in the creation of a major combat aircraft did not appear to hold much prospect of success in the first part of the 1960s. The fact that it eventually happened says a

Below: This Jaguar GR.Mk 1 of No. 14 Squadron, RAF, is perfectly at home in the low-level role.
Below right: An early Jaguar GR.Mk 1 (without the later nose-mounted laser ranger) is seen on a sortie from RAF Lossiemouth.

great deal for those in both countries who realized the potential of Anglo-French collaboration and who worked tirelessly for its fruition.

It was helpful to the idea of co-operation between the UK and France that, in the early 1960s, the air staffs of both countries were examining their future requirements in several important areas, and one subject of particular interest was a need for a future advanced trainer. In France, such an aircraft was needed to take pupil pilots from the relatively simple Potez/Fouga Magister up to the far more advanced Dassault Mirage III, while British plans envisaged a replacement for both the Hawker Hunter and Folland/Hawker Siddeley Gnat as the RAF's next advanced trainer. The French intended to have their aircraft in service by around 1970, the British some years after that. Both countries were interested in the incorporation of a strike capability in the new design, France partly in order to replace older attack types soon to end their service lives.

French thinking along these lines eventually led in 1964 to

the drawing up of a specific requirement known as ECAT (Ecole de Combat et Appui Tactique, or trainer/strike aircraft). This requirement called for a relatively simple, principally subsonic aircraft, capable of Mach 0.9 at 200 ft (61 m), an operational radius of 288 miles (463 km), and the ability to operate if necessary from the many aero-club grass strips found throughout France. Five French companies (Breguet, Nord, Potez, Dassault, and Sud-Aviation) subsequently submitted designs to meet the requirement; of these, the Breguet Br.121 was chosen in early 1965. Five different models of the Br.121 were proposed, including specific trainer and tactical strike variants. The weapon-carrying capacity of the latter was to be some 1,301 lb (590 kg), which was an extremely small amount considering the current weapon load of the Jaguar.

While these French developments had been taking place, a similar situation had arisen on the other side of the Channel. The British requirements for an advanced trainer with a tactical role had been drawn up in AST

(Air Staff Target) 362. The design teams of several famous British companies, such as Hunting at Luton and English Electric at Warton (both subsequently components of the British Aircraft Corporation), duly got to work on proposals to meet this requirement. Although some of the designs which appeared at this time, such as the BAC P.45 supersonic strike-trainer, were of considerable interest, developments on the political front overtook this work and in the event a design to meet AST 362 was rejected.

The joint Anglo-French co-operation which eventually led to the Jaguar arose in large part from the initiative of the British and French governments of the day, particularly the former. By 1964, the Anglo-French Concorde had already existed for some time and had shown the constructive possibilities of collaboration between the two countries. In Whitehall, the prospect of improving the UK's future chances of joining the Common Market were seen as possibly being enhanced by further co-operation of this kind, and by the end of 1964 sufficient joint consultations between the respective government ministries and air staffs from the UK and France had been made to issue a common operational require-ment for a single aircraft to fulfil the joint needs of the respective air arms of the two countries. This was a major step towards producing a full joint Anglo-French project. Of the various suitable designs existing at that time, the Br.121 was eventually selected as the air-craft on which the new jointly-produced type would be based. After considerable discussion, a Memorandum of Understanding was signed by both governments on 17 May 1965; this covered the joint development of the Breguet design to fulfil the needs of both countries.

A milestone in the Jaguar story had thus been reached, and the project has never really looked back since. The French were now nominated as design leaders, and BAC was named as the British airframe partner. Partly to prevent any bad feeling on the British side as a result of the apparent French pre-dominance in the project, a wholly new aircraft was launched at the same time in which BAC would be the main partner; this was to have been a supersonic swing-wing type with much greater power than the Br.121. The project became known as the AFVG (Anglo-French Variable Geometry), but was eventually abandoned in 1967 when the French withdrew.

With the signing of the Memorandum of Understanding, representatives of the companies concerned were able to start formal discussions about the project. It is noteworthy that these and many subsequent meetings were pursued in a most cordial manner, rarely being marked by any serious differ-ences of opinion which otherwise could have ruined the programme.

Under the Memorandum of Understanding, a joint Anglo-French industrial company was to be formed to administer the design and manufacture of the aircraft, and in May 1966 a company was registered in France under the name SEPECAT (Société Européenne de Production de l'Avion d'Ecole Combat et d'Appui Tactique). SEPECAT was subsequently to be supervised by an Anglo-French management committee, the chairmanship of which was originally shared equally by M B.C. Vallières of Breguet and Mr F. W. (now Sir Frederick) Page of BAC's Preston Division. The committee was to have at its disposal the relevant design, technical, manufacturing, financial, and various admini-strative facilities of both Breguet

and BAC, as well as being able to receive all necessary contracts relating to the Jaguar. SEPECAT also functions as the company with which prospective foreign buyers can negotiate. Airframe contracts for the RAF and Armée de l'Air were to be issued by DTCA (the Direction Technique de Construction Aéronautique), which acted on the authority of both the British and French governments. Even before SEPECAT had been formally established, a name had been found for the aircraft which it was to produce. With the permission of the motor car manufacturer the name Jaguar was chosen, the designation Br.121 being dropped largely as a result of the considerable redesign which the French project was now to undergo, and the eventual formation of the new company to produce it.

The basic manufacturing and industrial provisions having been made, the vitally important business of altering the original Br.121 design to meet the requirements of both the participating countries could get under way. Of very great significance in aiding this process had been a provision included in the original joint Memorandum of Understanding of May 1965. For any aircraft manufacturer, a firm commitment by a govern-ment to purchase a specified number of aircraft even before that aircraft has taken to the air is a most important and reward-ing starting point. The memorandum had firmly committed the UK and France to the purchase of 300 aircraft between them, and this fact was an excellent starting point for the whole Jaguar programme.

The French, in line with their original requirements, had opted for 75 single-seat strike aircraft and 75 two-seat trainers. On the other hand, the British commit-ment was for 150 trainers, with no initial provision whatsoever

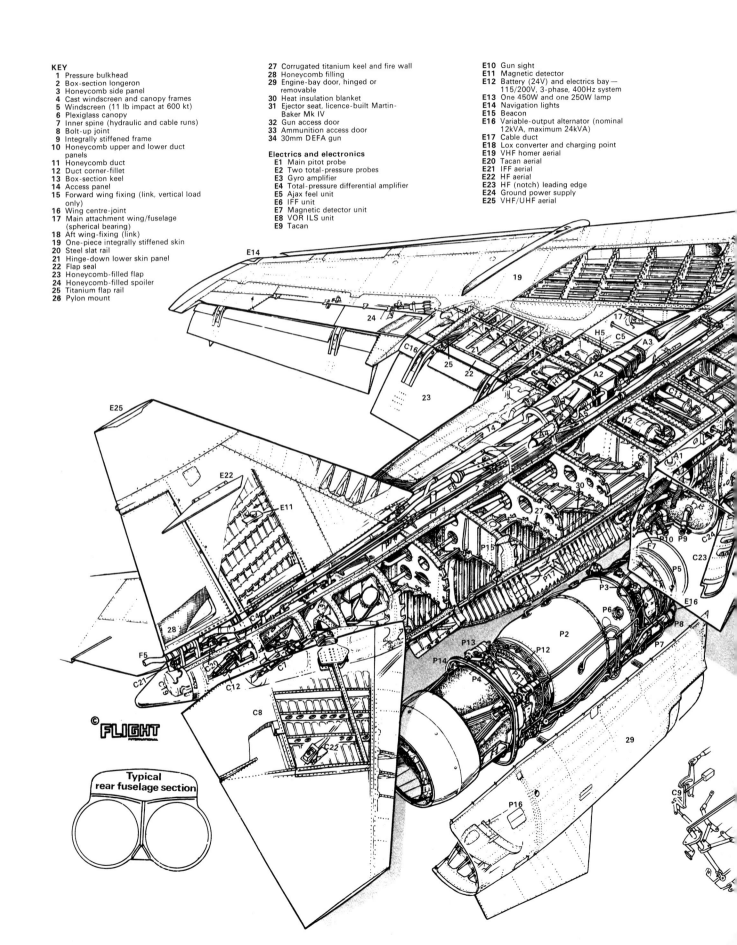

KEY

1 Pressure bulkhead
2 Box-section longeron
3 Honeycomb side panel
4 Cast windscreen and canopy frames
5 Windscreen (11 lb impact at 600 kt)
6 Plexiglass canopy
7 Inner spine (hydraulic and cable runs)
8 Bolt-up joint
9 Integrally stiffened frame
10 Honeycomb upper and lower duct panels
11 Honeycomb duct
12 Duct corner-fillet
13 Box-section keel
14 Access panel
15 Forward wing fixing (link, vertical load only)
16 Wing centre-joint
17 Main attachment wing/fuselage (spherical bearing)
18 Aft wing-fixing (link)
19 One-piece integrally stiffened skin
20 Steel slat rail
21 Hinge-down lower skin panel
22 Flap seal
23 Honeycomb-filled flap
24 Honeycomb-filled spoiler
25 Titanium flap rail
26 Pylon mount

27 Corrugated titanium keel and fire wall
28 Honeycomb filling
29 Engine-bay door, hinged or removable
30 Heat insulation blanket
31 Ejector seat, licence-built Martin-Baker Mk IV
32 Gun access door
33 Ammunition access door
34 30mm DEFA gun

Electrics and electronics
E1 Main pitot probe
E2 Two total-pressure probes
E3 Gyro amplifier
E4 Total-pressure differential amplifier
E5 Ajax feel unit
E6 IFF unit
E7 Magnetic detector unit
E8 VOR ILS unit
E9 Tacan

E10 Gun sight
E11 Magnetic detector
E12 Battery (24V) and electrics bay — 115/200V, 3-phase, 400Hz system
E13 One 450W and one 250W lamp
E14 Navigation lights
E15 Beacon
E16 Variable-output alternator (nominal 12kVA, maximum 24kVA)
E17 Cable duct
E18 Lox converter and charging point
E19 VHF homer aerial
E20 Tacan aerial
E21 IFF aerial
E22 HF aerial
E23 HF (notch) leading edge
E24 Ground power supply
E25 VHF/UHF aerial

© FLIGHT
INTERNATIONAL

Typical rear fuselage section

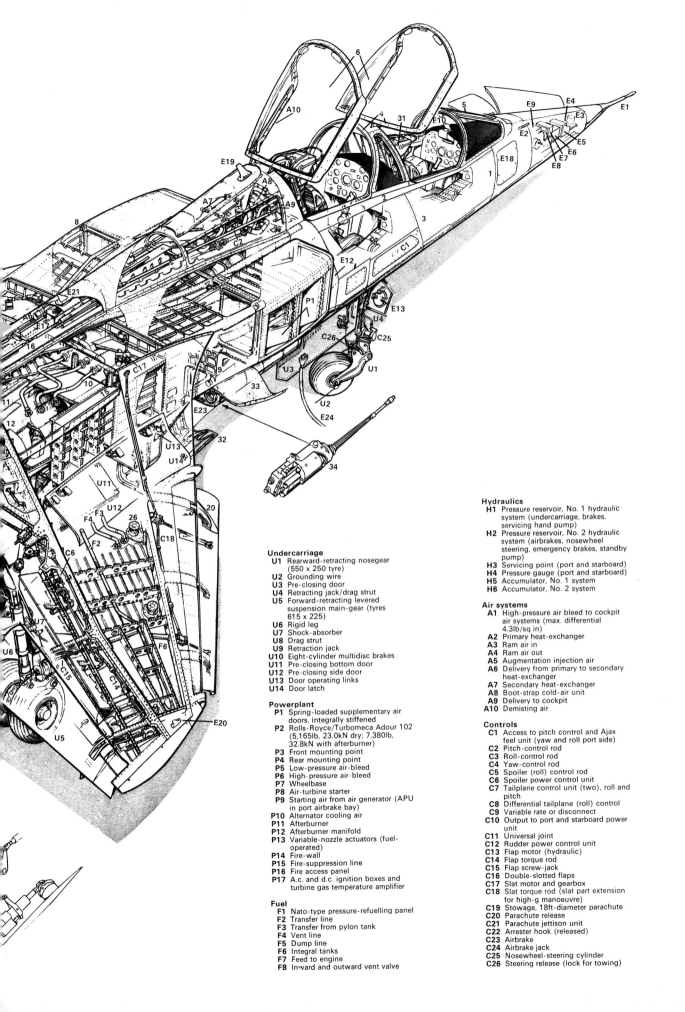

Undercarriage
U1 Rearward-retracting nosegear (550 x 250 tyre)
U2 Grounding wire
U3 Pre-closing door
U4 Retracting jack/drag strut
U5 Forward-retracting levered suspension main-gear (tyres 615 x 225)
U6 Rigid leg
U7 Shock-absorber
U8 Drag strut
U9 Retraction jack
U10 Eight-cylinder multidisc brakes
U11 Pre-closing bottom door
U12 Pre-closing side door
U13 Door operating links
U14 Door latch

Powerplant
P1 Spring-loaded supplementary air doors, integrally stiffened
P2 Rolls-Royce/Turbomeca Adour 102 (5,165lb, 23.0kN dry; 7,380lb, 32.8kN with afterburner)
P3 Front mounting point
P4 Rear mounting point
P5 Low-pressure air-bleed
P6 High-pressure air-bleed
P7 Wheelbase
P8 Air-turbine starter
P9 Starting air from air generator (APU in port airbrake bay)
P10 Alternator cooling air
P11 Afterburner
P12 Afterburner manifold
P13 Variable-nozzle actuators (fuel-operated)
P14 Fire-wall
P15 Fire-suppression line
P16 Fire access panel
P17 A.c. and d.c. ignition boxes and turbine gas temperature amplifier

Fuel
F1 Nato-type pressure-refuelling panel
F2 Transfer line
F3 Transfer from pylon tank
F4 Vent line
F5 Dump line
F6 Integral tanks
F7 Feed to engine
F8 Inward and outward vent valve

Hydraulics
H1 Pressure reservoir, No. 1 hydraulic system (undercarriage, brakes, servicing hand pump)
H2 Pressure reservoir, No. 2 hydraulic system (airbrakes, nosewheel steering, emergency brakes, standby pump)
H3 Servicing point (port and starboard)
H4 Pressure gauge (port and starboard)
H5 Accumulator, No. 1 system
H6 Accumulator, No. 2 system

Air systems
A1 High-pressure air bleed to cockpit air systems (max. differential 4.3lb/sq in)
A2 Primary heat-exchanger
A3 Ram air in
A4 Ram air out
A5 Augmentation injection air
A6 Delivery from primary to secondary heat-exchanger
A7 Secondary heat-exchanger
A8 Boot-strap cold-air unit
A9 Delivery to cockpit
A10 Demisting air

Controls
C1 Access to pitch control and Ajax feel unit (yaw and roll port side)
C2 Pitch-control rod
C3 Roll-control rod
C4 Yaw-control rod
C5 Spoiler (roll) control rod
C6 Spoiler power control unit
C7 Tailplane control unit (two), roll and pitch
C8 Differential tailplane (roll) control
C9 Variable rate or disconnect
C10 Output to port and starboard power unit
C11 Universal joint
C12 Rudder power control unit
C13 Flap motor (hydraulic)
C14 Flap torque rod
C15 Flap screw-jack
C16 Double-slotted flaps
C17 Slat motor and gearbox
C18 Slat torque rod (slat part extension for high-g manoeuvre)
C19 Stowage, 18ft-diameter parachute
C20 Parachute release
C21 Parachute jettison unit
C22 Arrester hook (released)
C23 Airbrake
C24 Airbrake jack
C25 Nosewheel-steering cylinder
C26 Steering release (lock for towing)

for a tactical variant intended for RAF service. Nevertheless, many of the changes which were incorporated into the original Breguet design during the summer and autumn of 1965, when the designers got down to definitive work, were sponsored by the British. An important requirement for the RAF was fully supersonic performance, and this resulted in such features as a redesign of the wing to incorporate a thinner section, while the fuselage was area-ruled and had its cross-section cut down in order to reduce drag. With increasing weight, resulting in part from the incorporation of the navigation and attack systems which the RAF wanted, the engine thrust had to be increased from that required by the Br.121. Extra power was also necessitated by the considerably increased weapon load, now envisaged as being some 10,000 lb (4,536 kg), a huge increase over the figure originally intended for the Br.121. Provision for a ferry range of 2,600 miles (4,185 km) was included, and the front fuselage was redesigned to give the two-seater's rear cockpit an improved line of sight for the instructor seated there. Detail internal changes were also incorporated, yet with all these alterations the external appearance of the

Jaguar remained similar to that of the Br.121. It was a consider-able achievement that the whole of this redesign work was achieved in a very short time, as the Jaguar's design was frozen in November 1965, a mere six months after full collaboration had started.

The Jaguar's powerplant was to be developed in a joint Anglo-French programme similar to that relating to the aircraft itself. Both governments had pointed out that only those engine manufacturers willing to co-operate with their counter-parts across the Channel would be in the running for selection in designing and building the required engines. To this end two joint companies were formed to compete for the Jaguar engine contract. Bristol Siddeley teamed up with the French company SNECMA (Société Nationale d'Etude et de

French Jaguar A aircraft operate in the close support and tactical nuclear roles, their range being extended by in-flight-refuelling support furnished by the Boeing C-135F aerial tankers.

Construction de Moteurs d'Aviation), although this pairing was unsuccessful. It was the Rolls-Royce and Turboméca link-up which was selected to produce the Jaguar's engines, a fact confirmed by the original Memorandum of Understanding of May 1965.

The successful Rolls-Royce and Turboméca engine combined the Rolls-Royce RB.172 turbo-fan with the Turboméca T-260 Turmolet engine. The RB.172 had been favoured by Breguet as the powerplant for the Br.121, and it was now altered to incorporate

In the close-support role, the Jaguar A can deliver useful quantities of conven-tional bombs with considerable accuracy despite its lack of the advanced British navigation/delivery system.

Common to British and French variants (a French Jaguar A is seen here) is the Irvin brake parachute, which has a diameter of 18 ft 0½ in (5.50 m) and is stowed in the tailcone.

parts of the Turmolet to produce an engine acceptable for the forthcoming Jaguar programme. The company formed to administer the creation and manufacture of the new engine was Rolls-Royce Turboméca Limited, which was registered in the UK during 1966. The engine was subsequently named Adour, after a French river, and parallel production lines were established at Derby in the UK and at Tarnos in France by Rolls-Royce and Turboméca respectively in order to produce the powerplant.

The exact number of Jaguars

The Jaguar As of EC 3/11 'Corse' are much used for inflight-refuelling practice, the reason being the wing's role as air-support unit for French army units on overseas posting.

to be procured by each country, while being spelled out in the original 1965 memorandum, was not in reality to be a final figure, and the following years saw significant changes in the direction of thinking with regard to the Jaguar's operational role. The most important changes in this respect came from the UK. The Jaguar had been regarded as purely a training aircraft by the RAF partly because of the expectation that several promising projects, such as the BAC TSR.2 and the Hawker Siddeley P.1154 V/STOL ground-attack fighter, would eventually be entering service. With the cancellation of these aircraft and the failure of the AFVG proposals, the RAF found itself short of a viable strike aircraft to fulfil its future needs. The Jaguar was a current and successful project which, with relative ease, could be developed into a strike air-

craft to meet such needs, and with this in mind the RAF procurement of Jaguars was altered to include a new British strike variant in addition to the existing British trainer variant. On 16 January 1967 an amendment to the original Memorandum of Understanding was included to this effect. The amendment also included an overall increase in the total number of Jaguars to be bought by the UK and France to 400 aircraft. Of the 200 aircraft now in the British order, 90 were to be of the new strike variant. The French commitment was revised at the same time. A new maritime variant intended for Aéronavale service was now included, 40 of these being included as well as an additional 10 two-seat trainers.

By the time that the first prototype Jaguars were well on their way to completion, five distinct variants of the aircraft were envisaged: the Jaguar A (for Appui) single-seat French strike model; the Jaguar E (Ecole) two-seat French trainer; the Jaguar M (Marin) single-seat French naval model; the Jaguar B (British) two-seat British trainer; and the Jaguar S (Strike) single-seat British strike model. Prototypes of each of these distinct variants were to fly as a prelude to full production of the Jaguar.

Jaguar prototypes

In total, eight prototypes were built to fulfil the Jaguar flight test programme. These consisted of five French and three British prototype Jaguars, and the subsequent test programme was fully integrated to ensure that as little duplication of effort as possible was made at any of the test centres in the UK and France.

The first prototype Jaguar to be completed was the first French prototype, the Jaguar E-01 two-seater. On 17 April 1968 it was rolled out for the start of ground tests and engine running at the Breguet factory at Vélizy-Villacoublay, near Paris. At the completion of this stage the aircraft was dismantled and shipped by road to the Centre d'Essais en Vol at Istres. The date for its maiden flight was subsequently held up for several weeks, partly as a result of the considerable unrest and civil strife which developed in France during the summer of 1968, when a state of near-revolution existed for a short time. It was not until 8 September 1968 that the Jaguar flew for the first time, when Bernard Witt, Breguet's chief test pilot, took to the air from Istres in Jaguar E-01. The first flight lasted just 25 minutes, but everything went very well and within the next few flights the aircraft had been flown supersonically and was soon being flown regularly by pilots from the Centre d'Essais en Vol, the Armée de l'Air, and by Jimmy Dell who was the then chief test pilot of BAC's Preston Division. Jaguar E-01 was subsequently used for aerodynamics and handling tests, and to check the correct functioning of the Jaguar's systems. The second Jaguar to fly was the second French prototype, Jaguar E-02, also a two-seater. This aircraft

first flew on 11 February 1969, again from Istres with Witt at the controls. It was later employed during the test programme for engine and flight performance testing.

On 29 March 1969 the first single-seat Jaguar, also a French prototype, made its first flight. This aircraft, Jaguar A-03, was followed into the air by the second French single-seat prototype, Jaguar A-04, on 27 May 1969; most of the French Jaguar prototypes were completed and flying sooner than their British counterparts, a situation later to be repeated with the initial production aircraft. Jaguar A-03 was used for evaluation and testing of the navigation and attack systems for the French attack Jaguars, while Jaguar A-04 pioneered weapon and stores carriage, and also performed weapon-firing trials. Both first flew from Istres, Jaguar A-03 with Witt at the controls and Jimmy Dell in Jaguar A-04, underlining the Anglo-French nature of the programme. The fifth and last French prototype for flight test was Jaguar M-05, which acted as prototype for the planned naval variant of the Jaguar. This last aircraft first flew during November 1969 in the hands of Breguet test pilot Jacques Jesberger.

One of the British prototypes had started its flight trials by this time, the single-seat Jaguar S prototype, Jaguar S-06 (XW560), making its first flight on 12 October 1969. The aircraft was flown at supersonic speed from BAC's airfield at Warton with Jimmy Dell at the controls. The second British single-seat prototype, Jaguar S-07 (XW563), first flew some time later in June 1970, again from Warton with the same test pilot. Jaguar S-06 subsequently

performed the British weapons trials, and tested the feasibility of inflight-refuelling for the Jaguar. Jaguar S-07 carried out the singularly important testing of the navigation and attack equipment to be installed in the production machines for the RAF. The eighth and final prototype, the British two-seat Jaguar B-08 (XW566), first flew from Warton on 30 August 1971 and was subsequently used for trials of the navigation and attack system as well as examining the utility of the two-seater's layout.

The various test programmes performed by the prototype Jaguars proved the effectiveness of the new aircraft, and most of the test project was performed without difficulty. A number of problems arose, however, although these were eventually overcome. A potentially serious difficulty concerned the early Adour engines. The first Adour had been successfully bench-tested at the Rolls-Royce facility at Derby on 9 May 1967, but there were several problems associated with the engine's thrust, especially when the afterburner was selected by the pilot. This was tending to have little or no effect at all until some 30 per cent of the afterburner power had been selected, and transition into afterburner power should have been smooth. The introduction of a part-throttle reheat system solved the difficulty after the Jaguar M-05 maritime prototype had been badly damaged in a heavy landing partly exacerbated by this thrust problem. Early examples of the engine also showed unacceptable fuel consumption, a problem which again was solved by the manufacturer. The engine difficulties arose partly because there had been no flying test-bed programme for the Adour, which would have led to the ironing out of these problems before the engine was fitted to the Jaguar. After these early

Above: One of the keys to the Jaguar's semi-STOL field performance and good low-level handling is the control system, with leading-edge slats, two-section double-slotted trailing-edge flaps and the fully-powered slab tailplane.

Below: The Jaguar is particularly well suited to the low-level role by its compact layout, as indicated by the three-view illustration of the Jaguar A, with (*bottom*) a side elevation of the Jaguar E.

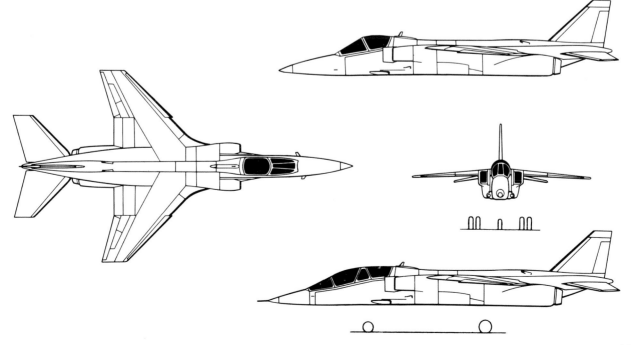

difficulties, the Adour became a very reliable and successful engine, being used to power the BAe Hawk as well as the Jaguar.

The first prototype, Jaguar E-01, was lost in an accident on 26 March 1970, although this did not detract from the test programme and the aircraft was not replaced.

As a backdrop to the successful testing of the prototype Jaguars, several developments had been taking place within the French aerospace industry which were to alter the Anglo-French relationship. In a significant move, Breguet had been merged with Avions Marcel Dassault as early as 1967, an action prompted by problems which Breguet had encountered in large part because of the decision of one of its major backers to pull out of the company. The merger with Dassault took full effect in 1971, and created a potentially new attitude on the French side which could raise a number of issues. Dassault had been one of the contenders in the original ECAT competition, and had not appreciated losing out to the winning Breguet design. The company possessed its own aircraft, such as the Mirage III

and F.1, some versions of which were to become rivals of the Jaguar for any future export sales. The paradox was thus created in which one of the partners in the Jaguar programme had become a potential competitor in any future attempts to sell the aircraft. With the Jaguar progressing very well by the start of the 1970s, however, the programme continued without any serious attempt from the French side to dismantle what was apparently going to be a very successful project.

Although the British intention, as expressed in the 1967 amendment to the original Memorandum of Understanding, had been to buy 110 trainer and 90 strike Jaguars, a further reassessment took place before full production of the Jaguar began. The October 1970 Defence White Paper pointed out that of the total of 200 Jaguars for the RAF, 165 would now be of the single-seat strike variant, with only 35 to be completed as trainers. In effect, this major change in emphasis completely stopped the use of the Jaguar as an advanced trainer in the RAF, for there simply would not be enough two-seat Jaguars to fulfil that

A mix of Jaguar GR.Mk 1s and T.Mk 2s awaiting delivery to the RAF displays the two types of forward fuselage.

role. In the event, the BAe Hawk eventually became the RAF's next advanced trainer, while the RAF two-seat Jaguars were to be used primarily as operational trainers for pilots who were posted to Jaguar squadrons.

A further major development in the Anglo-French requirement for the Jaguar took place when the planned naval variant for the French Aéronavale was cancelled. The maritime Jaguar had been intended as a Dassault Etendard IV replacement, and its various trials, including deck-landing trials at RAE Bedford and carrier suitability tests on board the French aircraft-carrier *Clemenceau*, had been largely successful. Instead, the French chose to look at other potential carrier-based aircraft, such as the McDonnell Douglas A-4 Skyhawk and Vought A-7 Corsair II from the United States, but finally opted for an improved model of the existing Etendard to meet their requirements: this is now in service as the Super Etendard. The Jaguar M was finally dropped in 1973, the whole maritime production allocation being added to the French air force procurement.

By the early 1970s the building of production Jaguars had started. This was partly as a result of the successful programme involving the prototype aircraft, although the initial agreement covering the construction of production Jaguars had been signed on 9 January 1968: this early date reflected the confidence of the British and French governments in the overall project. With the cancellation of the French maritime Jaguar, all production standard aircraft for the two countries were to be of the tactical (Jaguar A and S) and trainer (Jaguar B and E) variants only. Construction of the Jaguar was shared as fairly as possible between the British and French partners, the Dassault-Breguet factories at Biarritz and Toulouse constructing the aircraft's front and centre fuselage components while BAC's Military Aircraft Division built the rear fuselage, wings, tail unit and air inlets. A final assembly line was set up in each country, at Warton and Toulouse, where these various sections were mated together. Considerable emphasis had been placed on a relatively straightforward and simple design, a fact which aided this joint manufacturing programme.

The majority of the Jaguar's airframe is made of aluminium alloy, with titanium alloy used for panels in and around the engine bay areas. The airframe is stressed to 8.6 g limits, with a design maximum of 12 g indicating the robustness of the aircraft. Control surfaces are fully power-controlled, the power control systems being made by Fairey Hydraulics. As a weapons delivery platform the Jaguar is

greatly assisted by these controls, the aircraft being automatically stabilized by gyros which sense disturbances in flight and transmit appropriate correction instructions to the power control assemblies via a computer. This action is quite separate to any manoeuvring or other demands made by the pilot. On the ground, there is easy access for maintenance and overhaul of internal equipment by means of a large number of exterior panels which can be opened up to reveal the Jaguar's engines, internal systems and 'plumbing'. Underwing pylons, of which there are two per wing plus a centreline underfuselage pylon, are also readily accessible. The Jaguar stands relatively high off the ground, the landing gear and its distinctive wide low-pressure

tyres being dictated by requirements for a good rough field performance: for this reason Jaguars can operate away from prepared runways, and with a ground loading per square inch much lower than that on many other types, the Jaguar can even operate from road or motorway surfaces, all useful factors during possible times of crisis when normal air bases would be subject to attack and probable destruction.

It is the avionics, and specifically the navigation and attack equipment installed in the Jaguar, which above all else make the type a first-rate attack aircraft. In this area, however, are some of the major differences between the British and French variants of the Jaguar. Technically the most advanced (and most expensive)

The Jaguar M remains a fascinating 'might have been', a potentially decisive naval strike fighter cancelled for purely political reasons.

Below: An RAF Jaguar T.Mk 2 shows of the type's similarity to the single-seat Jaguar GR.Mk 1. The two crew are seated on Martin-Baker Mk 9 zero-zero ejector seats, the rear seat being raised by 15 in (38 cm) to provide the instructor with adequate forward vision.

Right: This view of the roll-out of a Jaguar T.Mk 2 gives an excellent impression of the sturdy landing gear, whose length provides good clearance for stores mounted under the fuselage centreline.

Left: Engine maintenance has never presented problems on the Jaguar, the semi-external location of the twin-engine powerplant, at easy height and with simply-detached access panels, permitting crews to work under optimum conditions, as on this hangared Jaguar GR.Mk 1.

Below: A Jaguar GR.Mk 1 unloads a 1,000-lb (454-kg) GP bomb during a training exercise. Note the 262-Imp gal (1,200-litre) drop tank under the fuselage.

Above right: Caught by the camera in the landing regime, the short-lived Jaguar E first prototype two-seater shows off many of the type's features, including the high-set and uncluttered wing able to carry a large weight of stores, the outward-canted twin ventral fins, the slab tailplane halves, the combination of leading-edge slats and double-slotted inboard and outboard trailing-edge flaps, and the fixed-geometry inlet with double spring-loaded secondary inlet doors.

Right: The second prototype Jaguar A single-seater shows off the clean lines of the type in the 'clean' condition with landing gear, flaps and slats retracted, and without stores under the wings and fuselage.

Above: The first two-seat Jaguar International for the Sultan of Oman's Air Force reveals the desert camouflage sported by No. 8 Squadron, based at Thumrayt for the ground-attack role with a secondary air-defence responsibility. Visible under the starboard wing is one of the two 1,200-litre (264-Imp gal) drop tanks that can be carried on the inboard underwing hardpoints. The type has seen action in the counter-insurgency role, and a second squadron of Jaguar Internationals was formed at Masirah during 1984.

Left: The Jaguar GR.Mk 1 can combine range with offensive punch, this example carrying a centreline 1,200-litre (264-Imp gal) tank plus (under the port wing) two 1,000-lb (454-kg) bombs in tandem (inboard hardpoint) and two Matra Type 155 pods of 68-mm (2.68-in) SNEB rockets (outboard hardpoint).

Right: The cockpit of the Jaguar is excellently designed from an ergonomic aspect. The key items (apart from the standard flight, communication and engine instruments) are the Ferranti FIN 1064 digital inertial navigation and weapon-aiming system with its circular display, and the Smiths' diffractive-optics head-up display (top). The latter uses a low-light-level TV camera, and in comparison with the standard refractive-optics HUD offers the pilot a wider field of vision, improved optical characteristics and a brighter display.

Below: Extensive areas of removable panelling make engine maintenance relatively simple, as can be seen in this illustration of a Jaguar GR.Mk 1 (the 37th item from the second production batch) of No. 226 Operational Conversion Unit, normally based at Lossiemouth. The long fore-and-aft box on the fin above the projecting VOR aerial is the Marconi Space and Defence Systems ARI.18223 radar warning receiver.

The second prototype Jaguar S was built by the English Electric Division of the British Aircraft Corporation at Warton (Lancs), and here reveals some of its load-carrying ability, with three 1,000-lb (454-kg) retarded bombs and four Hunting BL755 600-lb (272-kg) cluster bombs. The latter is a particularly important weapon for low-level attacks on small targets (hard and soft), and scatters 147 bomblets for a high kill probability.
Inset left: A French air force Jaguar A fires an Aérospatiale AS.30L air-to-surface missile with the aid of a Martin-Marietta/Thomson-CSF ATLIS II laser-designator pod, seen with its nose shield raised on the centreline hardpoint.
Inset top: Jaguar GR.Mk 1 of No. 14 Squadron, RAF, seen in flight. The squadron is part of RAF Germany and based at Brüggen.

Above: Pending the delivery of her Jaguar International aircraft, India was loaned 18 Jaguars by the RAF, including these two aircraft, namely a Jaguar GR.Mk 1 (background) and a Jaguar T.Mk 2 (foreground). The first loaned aircraft were handed over in July 1979.

Left: Seen on test at the Rolls-Royce test facility at Derby is an afterburning Adour turbofan, which in the Jaguar has proved itself most reliable and offering the twin advantages of low specific fuel consumption with high power-to-weight ratio.

Above right: A Jaguar GR.Mk 1 of No. 2 Squadron, RAF Germany, flies close to Mount Etna in Italy while on detachment from its normal base at Laarbruch. This aircraft is the 29th item from the third production batch.

Right: The only Jaguar variant not to have entered production so far is the Jaguar M carrierborne model developed for the French navy, and seen here during trials aboard the carrier *Clemenceau* before being cancelled in favour of the Dassault Super Etendard.

Above: Two of Ecuador's 10 single-seat Jaguar Internationals are seen at take-off. Ecuador's 'hot and high' climatic and geographical situation presents no problem to these up-engined aircraft. The Ecuadorean order was fulfilled during the course of 1977.

Inset left: Nose-on view of a Jaguar T.Mk 2 of the Empire Test Pilots School at Boscombe Down.
Below: The Jaguar FBW incorporates the UK's first quadruplex fly-by-wire control system, and lacks any form of alternative control as the FBW system is so reliable.

model is the British Jaguar S, which was to enter service as the Jaguar GR.Mk 1. The British two-seat Jaguar B carries much of the GR.Mk 1's navigation and attack equipment, this variant entering service as the Jaguar T.Mk 2. Included amongst the standard avionics fit are VHF/UHF and HF radio, ILS (Instrument Landing System), IFF (Identification Friend or Foe), Tacan, Smiths Industries HUD (Head-Up Display) and HSI (Horizontal Situation Indicator), and the centrally important Marconi Avionics digital/inertial navigation and weapon aiming subsystem (NAVWASS). This last includes an MCS 920M digital computer, three-gyro inertial platform, inertial velocity sensor, Navigation Control Unit (NCU), and Projected Map Display (PMD). The NAVWASS is the heart of the RAF Jaguar's attack avionics, and is one of the most advanced systems of its kind ever to fly in a combat aircraft. The Jaguar GR.Mk 1 added to this a Ferranti laser ranger and marked-target seeker housed in the front fuselage, giving it its distinctive chisel-shaped nose. The Jaguar GR.Mk 1 also includes a fin-mounted ECM and sensor pod not found on other British and French Jaguars. There is provision for inflight-refuelling. Both the British models are fitted with Martin-Baker Mk 9 ejector seats, much better units than their French counterparts because of their zero-altitude, zero-speed firing capability.

The French two-seat Jaguar E's internal equipment includes VHF/UHF radio, VOR/ILS, IFF, Tacan, a twin-gyro inertial plat-form, an air-data computer system, and a CSF 121 fire-control sighting unit/weapon selector. In addition to these features, the Jaguar A includes a panoramic camera, Decca RDN 72 Doppler radar, Crouzet Type 90 navigation computer and

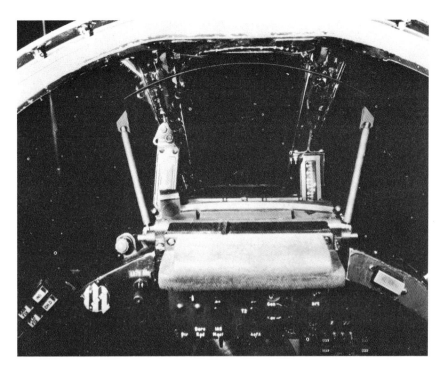

Above: The Smiths Industries head-up display is a key feature in the Jaguar in British service. The HUD projects into the pilot's line of sight all vital attack and flight information, focussed at infinity.

Below: The head-up display does not materially affect the pilot's forward field of vision, as this sight from the rear seat of a Jaguar T.Mk 2 indicates. This is vital in high-speed low-level flight.

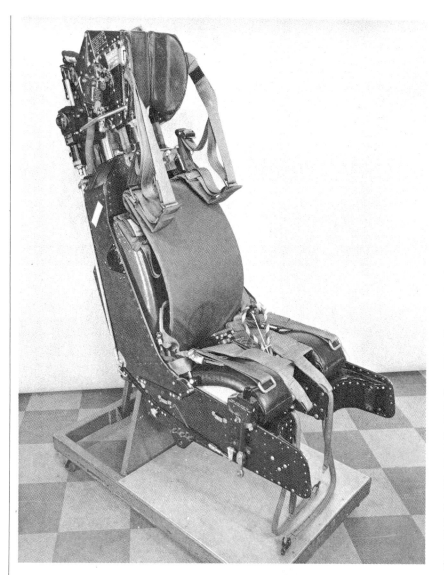

and 7,305-lb (3,313-kg) thrust with afterburner. Total internal fuel capacity was 264-Imp gal (4,200 litres). The Jaguar's fuel system is armoured in important and vulnerable sections to prevent damage from groundfire. A typical attack radius with internal fuel on a lo-lo-lo (all low-level flying) mission is 357 miles (575 km), a range extended to 519 miles (835 km) for the same type mission with external fuel.

On completion, some of the initial production Jaguars were delegated to the flying-test programmes, early French production Jaguars joining the French prototypes at Istres, while some of the early British-assembled production aircraft found their way to the Aeroplane and Armament Experimental Establishment (A&AEE) at Boscombe Down. The first production Jaguar to fly was the French two-seat Jaguar E-1, which made its first flight on 2 November 1971 with Bernard Witt at the controls. The initial British production aircraft first flew on 11 October the following year. It was a Jaguar GR.Mk 1, bearing the designation Jaguar S-1 although it was also assigned the military serial number XX108. The first production Jaguar T.Mk 2 (XX136) made its maiden flight on 28 March 1973. The 'chisel-nose' initially appeared on the second British production Jaguar GR.Mk 1 (XX109), which took to the air in November 1972; some of the early Jaguar GR.Mk 1s were delivered without the laser nose and tail ECM fairing. With production aircraft thus coming off the assembly lines at an ever-increasing rate, the Jaguar was nearing its service debut.

target selector, passive radar-warning equipment, a CSF 31 weapon-aiming computer, and a Dassault fire-control computer for Martel anti-radar weapons. included, with Martin-Baker Mk 4 Inflight-refuelling provision is ejector seats capable of zero-altitude operation but only at speeds down to 104 mph (167 km/h).

Internally-carried armament for the Jaguar GR.Mk 1 consists of two 30-mm Aden cannon, one on each side of the lower fuselage below the cockpit. The Jaguar E and Jaguar S each have a similar provision, but for 30-mm DEFA cannon; however, the British Jaguar T.Mk 2 has only a single 30-mm Aden cannon in the lower port fuselage. Maximum external stores load is some 10,000 lb (4,536 kg). The two-seat variants have a similar weapons-carrying capability to the strike models, and can be used as necessary in operational missions. All Jaguars are powered by the Adour engine, which has afterburning capability in all the variants. The initial model of this engine fitted in production Jaguars was the Adour Mk 102, capable of 5,115-lb (2,320-kg) thrust dry

Into service

The Jaguar gained operational status first with the French Armée de l'Air. As early as 1968 that air force's 7eme Escadre (an *Escadre* is roughly equivalent to a Wing in the RAF) had been selected to be the first operational unit to receive the Jaguar, and preparations for service entry had begun in earnest at the start of the 1970s. In February 1973 the training of ground crews from the 7eme Escadre began with a course of instruction and practical training on Jaguars operated by the CEAM (Centre d'Expériences Aériennes Mili-

taires) at Mont de Marsan, which had received its first Jaguar on 4 May 1972. Training of flight crews began during March of 1973, part of the training taking the form of practical flying instruction in some of the establishment's two-seater Jaguar Es.

On 19 June 1973 the Jaguar officially entered squadron service, Escadron 1/7 'Provence' being the first operational unit. Considerable ceremony marked the event, the then Minister of the Armed Forces, Robert Galley, and the chief of the French air staff, Général Claude Grigaut, being amongst the dignitaries in attendance. The unit was based at St Dizier, which only a few earlier had become the home

base of the 7eme Escadre. The Jaguar represented a massive leap forward when compared to the unit's previous equipment, the Dassault Mystère IVA, which had been a capable type in its time but which, by the 1970s, was very much the product of a previous generation of combat aircraft. Général Grigaut delivered an address at the event which went some way towards expressing the attitude towards the Jaguar of those within the Armée de l'Air associated with it. The general opinion was that the Jaguar was proving to be an exceptionally fine strike aircraft, capable of carrying an impress. payload over greater distances than those attainable by other French combat aircraft of that

The nosewheel unit (in this instance of a Jaguar E two-seater) is steerable and of Messier design with a Dunlop wheel and low-pressure tyre for rough-field operation. Note the twin landing lights incorporated in the door.

type, and with the possibility of great accuracy in weapon delivery. So the French were very pleased with the Jaguar, even though at a cost of around £1 million each

aircraft was rather more expensive than the price originally envisaged for the Br.121.

While other French units began the transition to operational

RAF Coltishall groundcrew rush a fuelling hose to a Jaguar during quick-turnround practice.
An impressive line-up of No. 6 Squadron Jaguar GR.Mk 1 aircraft at RAF Lossiemouth in 1974.

A Jaguar GR.Mk 1 of No. 54 squadron sorties over the North Sea with an external load of two 264-Imp gal (1,200-litre) drop tanks and four 1,000-lb (454-kg) bombs, two on the centreline hard-point under the fuselage and one each on the outer underwing hardpoints. Note the 'chisel nose' laser ranger/seeker.

status on the Jaguar, the type was nearing its entry into RAF service. The first production Jaguar to reach the RAF was delivered on 30 May 1973, Jaguar S-4 (XX111) arriving at RAF Lossiemouth in Scotland to begin the process of ground crew training. The Jaguar Operational Conversion Unit (JOCU) was established at Lossiemouth from March 1973 onwards; it would receive the first production Jaguars for the RAF and act as the training unit

for the type. Single-seat Jaguars XX114 and XX115 were delivered to the JOCU on 13 September 1973, marking the start of official deliveries to the RAF. The JOCU was eventually redesignated No. 226 OCU in late 1974, taking on the identity of the former English Electric/BAC Lightning OCU.

The RAF's first operational Jaguar squadron was No. 54 Squadron. This unit had re-formed at Lossiemouth on 29 March 1974 to receive the Jaguar, and at a ceremony held at this airfield on 5 June of that year, the squadron officially entered service with the Jaguar. The ceremony was marked by speeches from several important RAF officers, including Air Chief Marshal Sir Denis Smallwood, Air Officer Commanding-in-Chief

RAF Strike Command. Like its French counterpart, the RAF was full of praise for the Jaguar. The aircraft's attack capability was especially praised and recognized as being second to none in the RAF inventory, improving its strike capability by a considerable amount. In August 1974, No. 54 Squadron moved from the training base at Lossiemouth to the fully operational airfield at Coltishall in Norfolk. It became operational and completely combat-ready on 1 January 1975. Coltishall was to become the home of all the UK-based operational Jaguar units, and it was not long before the type was entering widespread RAF service in squadrons based in West Germany as well as in the UK.

RAF employment

The total number of Jaguars procured for British service eventually reached some 203 examples, which is a slight increase over the original intended figure of 200. The extra three aircraft are all Jaguar T.Mk 2s, added to original procurement and destined for service with the Empire Test Pilots School at the A&AEE Boscombe Down, and the Institute of Aviation Medicine at RAE Farnborough. This makes a grand total of 38 Jaguar T.Mk 2s, while the full complement of 165 Jaguar GR.Mk 1s, as first mentioned in the Defence White Paper of 1970, was built without increment. Apart from No. 226 OCU at Lossiemouth, the Jaguar was to eventually equip eight front-line operational squadrons of the RAF: three based in the UK, and five in West Germany as a part of the RAF's commitment to NATO air power on the European mainland.

Following the re-equipment of No. 54 Squadron with Jaguars, other squadrons soon began the transition to the type. The RAF's second Jaguar unit was No. 6 Squadron, which re-formed at Lossiemouth on 30 September 1974 and moved south to Coltishall during November. These two units, plus No. 41 Squadron which re-formed at Coltishall on 1 April 1977, formed the total UK-based complement of Jaguar operational squadrons. Of the three, No. 41 has the primary function of tactical reconnaissance, and is one of the two RAF Jaguar units with this specific role. All three Coltishall Jaguar squadrons are assigned to No. 1 Group, RAF Strike Command. This group contains the UK-based strike and tactical squadrons of the RAF,

other squadrons under its jurisdiction being equipped with the BAe Harrier GR.Mk 3 and the Panavia Tornado GR.Mk 1. The group has a rapid overseas deployment capability, and maintains a fleet of transport aircraft which, in time of emergency, would be used to move the strike squadrons' ground personnel and equipment to the European bases where the squadrons would be deployed.

The remaining five operational Jaguar squadrons are a part of RAF Germany, four of these (Nos 14, 17, 20, and 31) in the strike role while the fifth, No. 2 Squadron, carries out tactical reconnaissance as its primary task. The Jaguar has been the most numerous type in RAF Germany for some time; it is partnered in the strike role within this organization by smaller numbers of the Harrier

The Jaguar T.Mk 2 (seen here in the markings of No. 41 Squadron from RAF Coltishall) retains combat capability though lacking the laser nose.

Below: Jaguar GR.Mk 1s from RAF Bruggen formate over West Germany, an area in which they have vital responsibilities.
Below left: Two Jaguar GR.Mk 1s of No. 20 Squadron pull a tight turn over a German *Schloss* during a training sortie.
Below right: Hardened hangars such as this at RAF Bruggen provide base defence for aircraft like this cluster bomb-loaded Jaguar GR.Mk 1 of No. 14 Squadron.

GR.Mk 3, Blackburn/HS/BAe Buccaneer S.Mk 2B and, from the early 1980s, the Tornado GR.Mk 1. All four of the strike Jaguar squadrons are based at Brüggen, the only operational RAF type to operate from this West German airfield, while No. 2 Squadron is based at Laarbruch. The first of the Jaguar squadrons intended for RAF Germany, No. 14 Squadron, was re-formed in the first half of 1975, being operational by the end of the year. It was followed by No. 17

and then No. 31 Squadron, with Nos. 2 and 20 Squadrons receiving their initial Jaguars during 1976. With increasing deliveries of production Jaguar GR.Mk 1s, the full complement of Jaguar squadrons was able to build up relatively smoothly, and by 1978 all production Jaguar GR.Mk 1s had been completed and handed over to the RAF.

The airfields at Brüggen and Laarbruch are situated close to the Dutch border, the Jaguars being based this far west in

keeping with the philosophy which places most British, US and Canadian front-line units in West Germany well back from the border with East Germany; this is because any Soviet armed thrust into West Germany would most probably overwhelm units based close to the East German border before any effective countermeasures could be taken. All units of RAF Germany are included within a larger administrative organization, 2nd Allied Tactical Air Force. This air

A Jaguar GR.Mk 1 of No. 2 Squadron, RAF Germany, swings past a German radar site. Note the underfuselage reconnaissance pod.

force comprises, as well as the RAF contingent, units from various NATO countries including the United States. The RAF Germany units represent a considerable fighting force whose Jaguars have established themselves as a vitally important part of its strike element.

With the exception of No. 20 Squadron, which had formerly flown the Harrier, all the RAF Jaguar squadrons had previously been equipped with the McDonnell Douglas Phantom. The advent of the Jaguar effectively freed the Phantom from the strike and tactical reconnaissance roles to which it had previously been assigned, allowing it to be used in the future for air-defence duties. Although the US-built Phantom has a useful strike capability, as demonstrated by US forces during the Vietnam War, the Jaguar is a much more dedicated and sophisticated attack aircraft,

and the Phantom became of greater use to the RAF in a fighter role.

In order to perform their strike mission, RAF Jaguars are cleared for a variety of weapons quite apart from their built-in 30-mm cannon. A common strike ordnance carried by Jaguars in RAF service are 1,000-lb (454-kg) bombs, which can be carried on all the Jaguar's stores pylons under the wings and fuselage, although the inner-wing pylons are often used to carry 264-Imp gal (1,200-litre) fuel drop tanks; these pylons are cleared for greater load-carrying than the outer-wing pylons. The 1,000-lb (454-kg) bombs can be of the free-fall, retarded, or laser-guided variety. The last-mentioned are capable of use with the laser equipment carried in the nose of the Jaguar GR.Mk 1. Cluster bombs, including the Hunting BL 755 variety, are also included in the Jaguar's possible

weapons load, in addition to other sizes of bombs, SNEB rocket pods and associated hardware. The most potentially destructive of all weapons carried by the RAF's Jaguars are the tactical nuclear weapons available for use in times of great crisis, a subject which retains a considerable cloak of secrecy. For self-defence, the possibility exists for the carriage of Sidewinder air-to-air dogfighting missiles. The ability to carry the Sidewinder is a more recent development, having come to the fore towards the end of the 1970s after being pioneered in part by the export Jaguar International. Although the Jaguar is fully capable of carrying these missiles, their employment by the RAF has not been as extensive as in some overseas countries using the aircraft.

The means by which the RAF Jaguar delivers strike ordnance onto its target sets it apart from many other strike aircraft, and the navigation and attack avionics fitted in the Jaguar are sufficiently capable of performing their relevant functions so that one crew member can operate them and fly the aircraft at the same time. The various components of the NAVWASS are extremely sophisticated pieces of equipment, and a typical Jaguar mission is based to a very large extent on the workings of the NAVWASS and the information which it supplies to the pilot; but it is able to do this only if as much relevant information as possible is fed into it at the start of the flight. Preparation is therefore necessary before each flight, the pre-flight briefing being of great significance. After receiving the relevant information at this briefing, the pilot then has to set the navigation and attack

Above: The Jaguar series can carry a truly diverse weapon load, as indicated by the display of a Jaguar International at the Farnborough air display in 1976. Particularly notable is the overwing Sidewinder air-to-air missile fit, and other potent weapons are the Martel anti-radar missile, the Exocet anti-ship missile, the Durandal runway-cratering munition, and the parachute-retarded bombs.

Right: The Jaguar is cleared for a wide range of conventional munitions, but the most frequently used are unguided rockets and free-fall bombs, the latter type being in evidence during this rearming exercise at RAF Coltishall during 1977 in the form of a 1,000-lb (454-kg) retarded bomb.

An inert Sidewinder air-to-air missile is seen under the starboard wing of an RAF Jaguar GR.Mk 1 during clearance trials for this weapon. Also show to advantage are the two-piece double-slotted trailing-edge flaps.

system in accordance with the flight information. Before boarding the aircraft, he enters details of the weapon load being carried on a set of indicators inside the aircraft's nosewheel compartment. The weapons control panel inside the cockpit is then checked to ensure that it has also recorded this information, which is necessary in order to ensure that the optimum release is selected for the hardware when the target is reached.

The pre-flight routine then continues with the readying of the Marconi E3R inertial platform, the aircraft's exact position of take-off in latitude and longitude, the height above sea level and the magnetic variation all being inserted. The Sperry gyro-magnetic compass is then swung to true heading for synchronization; this is necessary because a magnetic reading is impossible with all the metal in and around the aircraft. The true

heading is usually achieved by aligning the aircraft with a painted (and thus fixed-bearing) guideline on the floor of its parking area. All known details of the mission to be flown, obtained by the pilot at the pre-flight briefing, are inserted into the MCS 920M computer, including details of the turning or way points, initial point (IP) and target(s). When all the systems have been switched on, (some of which have a long warm-up time, one being the HUD) the pilot can then start the engines.

A Micro-Turbo air generator self-starter is employed for this purpose, and as soon as the aircraft is ready to roll the pilot can then select the NAV phase on the Navigation Control Unit (NCU). This has the effect of selecting the co-ordinates of the first turning point programmed for the mission. The HUD, Horizontal Situation Indicator (HSI), and Projected Map Display (PMD) all represent this information for pilot reference after take-off. For most of the mission the pilot uses the readings given to him by these instruments, the HUD projecting all relevant flight information directly into his line of sight as he flies the aircraft. The PMD does exactly as its name suggests, and can show the programmed locations of the turning points, IPs and targets, and the direction to these points. The pilot usually carries an old-fashioned hand-held map as well, as a back-up in case the navigation equipment fails altogether or (for whatever reason) fails to give the correct information. The HSI gives the pilot a digital read-out of the distance to each turning point in relation to the aircraft's position, as well as details of the planned track to each turning point. All this explains the crucial importance of knowing the exact co-ordinates of these points before the mission begins, so that they can be fed into the NAVWASS.

When the aircraft comes to within two minutes of each turning point on its journey, the HUD automatically changes from navigation mode to close navigation or, if the target is being approached, into attack mode. The pilot is shown visually the exact position of each turning point by an X marker on the HUD. The two major types of attack open to the Jaguar are

the planned attack and the target of opportunity attack. The mode of attack chosen by the pilot is fed into the Weapons Aiming Mode Selector (WAMS). The planned attack is made against a target whose position was known before the Jaguar took off so that it could be fed into the computer. All relevant attack details are shown on the HUD as the pilot flies the aircraft towards the target, taking instructions from his navigation equipment. When the IP is reached the Jaguar turns from that point onto the run-in to the target, the HUD displaying its attack symbols, a drift-compensated bomb line with a target bar showing the continuously computed impact point of the weapons chosen for the attack. The aircraft is flown so that the target, when visually sighted, is kept on the bomb line, the target bar being moved by means of an up/down switch by the pilot so that the target coincides with it to give range information. Weapon release, when the correct range is reached, is automatic although the pilot depresses a fire-commital button until the weapons are released.

The accuracy of this system is enhanced by means of the laser ranger and marked-target seeker in the nose. Using the laser ranger, the pilot obtains accurate range information by using the target bar to direct the laser as he flies towards the target, the very accurate range details thus obtained being fed directly into the weapon system. Additionally, the whole laser system with its marked-target seeker can be used in conjunction with laser designators operated by ground forces. In this attack mode, the aircraft is flown towards the area of the target with the marked-target seeker ready to pick up returns of laser energy from the target, which is illuminated by the ground forces or a forward

air controller. As soon as returns are detected, the marked-target seeker locks onto the target. Automatic ranging is then provided by the equipment in preparation for the automatic weapon release when the correct range is reached.

If a target of opportunity attack is being made, much the same procedure can be used as in a planned attack except that the position of the target is not known before the flight begins. Nevertheless, a fully computed attack can still be made. TGT OPP attack mode is selected by the pilot on the WAMS, which immediately causes the attack symbols to appear on the HUD, albeit without an X marker to show the target because the position of the target is unknown to the system. (A facility has existed in which a pilot can plot the co-ordinates of a target during flight for the NAVWASS, which involved flying over the target or a suitable IP nearby and pressing a regress store key when directly overhead, this having the effect of introducing the exact position of the target or IP into the aircraft's computer.) In the TGT OPP attack the pilot has to provide full ranging and tracking information for the attack system, including use of the target bar on the HUD for ranging. The laser ranging equipment can also be used for accurate ranging if this is available. (The Jaguar T.Mk 2 used in this type of attack would not have the use of the laser equipment.)

As soon as an attack has been made, the whole system reverts to the navigation mode with the relevant symbols displayed on the HUD. Attacks against a number of targets can be made during a single sortie if necessary; unless a major failure occurs within the avionics, the navigation and attack system is able to provide the same level of information for each providing that it was programmed correctly at the start.

With such a large amount of electronic and computer equipment on board, occasional failures of part of the systems can take place. However, provision has been made so that in such an event the pilot can be shown as soon as possible that the information being displayed to him is erroneous; he can then attempt to discover which part of the system has failed, and decide on the basis of this whether or not to proceed on the mission using any of the back-up systems available.

Conventional attacks using the Jaguar's navigation and attack equipment are always planned for more than one aircraft, a typical attack mission being flown by four aircraft, although formations of two are also possible. This means a great deal of training in formation flying, and in providing the mutual defence required in such an attack profile.

If a formation attack is being made, the order in which each aircraft attacks its designated target is crucial to the success of any mission, and such details are always given at the all-important pre-flight briefing. If all the aircraft arrived over the target either timed too close together or at the same time, the results could be catastrophic, with aircraft flying into the explosions of each other's weapons. The speeds at which attacks are made would generally be in the high subsonic range, rather than supersonic. Flying at subsonic speed allows the aircraft to fly closer to the ground and with greater safety than would be possible at supersonic speeds, since it is more important to fly low so that the enemy's defences can be avoided. In wartime attack missions would be flown at or below 250 ft (76 m); training flights are normally flown at or above this height to avoid creating too much disturbance in peacetime. Such low-level flying demands a great deal of concentration from pilots, but with the Jaguar's navigation and attack system partially reducing pilot workload there is some time available to keep a watch outside the cockpit, which is also useful in reducing

Fuelled but unarmed, a pair of Jaguar GR.Mk 1 aircraft stand ready to go (external power plugged in) at RAF Leuchars during 1978.

the chance of being surprised by enemy fighters. Attack missions flown with tactical nuclear weapons differ from conventional attacks in that, in this case, Jaguars would work singly, usually undertaking the destruction of a single target.

With their impressive attack capability, RAF Jaguars have excelled in various overseas and NATO weapons meets and competitions. Amongst the most important of these have been participation in exercises on the other side of the Atlantic in Canada and the United States. Pioneers in the Jaguar's involvement were aircraft from No. 20 Squadron, which took part in Exercise Maple Flag at the Canadian Armed Forces Base at Cold Lake, Alberta in 1980. In partnership with No. 6 Squadron, Jaguars from No. 20 consistently scored higher successes than their opponents during the exercise, the opposition including examples of Canadian Armed

Hardened shelters provide full servicing capabilities for pairs of Jaguars, such as these two Jaguar GR.Mk 1s of No. 6 Squadron normally *rased* at RAF Coltishall. Note the fuel dump tube below the fin of the nearer aircraft.

Forces front-line aircraft and US Air Force McDonnell Douglas F-15 Eagles. This success was followed up by No. 54 Squadron at Exercise Red Flag later in the year. Red Flag is held at Nellis Air Force Base in Nevada, and is an annual exercise demanding a great deal from both aircraft and pilots. On this occasion too the Jaguar proved itself as a thoroughly capable attack aircraft, much to the envy of many participating US Air Force personnel; this fact was demonstrated again at subsequent Red Flag meetings.

Within NATO, RAF Jaguars have had important successes at various weapons competitions. These include victories at the biennial Tactical Air Meet at Ramstein in West Germany. Particularly noteworthy was the June/July meeting in 1980, when No. 31 Squadron won no less than two of the coveted attack awards, the Canberra Trophy for retarded bombing at low altitude, and the Broadhurst Trophy for conventional bombing. One of the squadron's pilots, Flight Lieutenant Ian Kenvyn, managed to score a maximum 400 points during the competition, while five other Jaguar pilots each scored 380 points, a remarkable achievement. Jaguars have won other major honors in such competitions as the Salmond Trophy, a navigation and bombing meet within RAF Germany.

Jaguars have often beaten Harriers and Buccaneers in this competition, the first of many successes being gained by No. 14 Squadron in 1975, the first year in which the Jaguar was eligible to compete.

The introduction of a tactical reconnaissance role for the Jaguar necessitated the design and construction of a purpose-built reconnaissance pod to be carried externally, there being little or no room within the Jaguar's tightly-packed interior for the range of sensors and cameras needed to fulfil this role. Adopted to meet the requirement was a pod designed and built by British Aerospace, which carries a variety of cameras and infra-red equipment. For daylight photography, cameras giving horizon-to-horizon coverage are installed in two rotating drums inside the pod. The forward drum contains two low oblique-across-track

Left: The BAe reconnaissance pod carries in its rear an HS 401 linescan IR set for night and poor weather information gathering.
Below left: RAF groundcrew change the film in a Jaguar's reconnaissance pod between sorties.

best route over or around the target to gain maximum photographic coverage. A great advantage of having the cameras linked to the NAVWASS equipment is that each photographic frame is marked with its exact latitude and longitude. This gives precise information about locations of targets, which can be fed into the NAVWASS of attack Jaguars before missions. Both Nos 2 and 41 Squadrons employ the reconnaissance pod, although each retains a limited strike capability in addition to its primary task of tactical reconnaissance.

In line with the continuing process of updating service equipment, the RAF is having its Jaguars progressively fitted with new or improved systems and hardware. A major alteration concerns the navigation and attack equipment, parts of which are being replaced by Ferranti FIN 1064 digital inertial navigation and weapons aiming equipment. This was first flown in a Jaguar on 31 July 1981, and will increase the effectiveness and accuracy of the exceptionally competent NAVWASS equipment currently installed in operational aircraft. RAF Jaguars have also been retrofitted with improved Adour engines; the Adour Mk 104 of 5,320-lb (2,410-kg) thrust dry and 8,040-lb (3,645-kg) thrust with afterburner has been installed in place of the earlier Adour Mk 102. Such improvements maintain the Jaguar as one of the RAF's most potent warplanes, and although a restructuring of the Jaguar force is likely in the future, the aircraft has played a vital role within the RAF's strike inventory for almost a decade.

Vinten F95 Mk 10 cameras and one forward-looking oblique F95 Mk 7 camera for medium- and low-altitude missions; the rear drum can be fitted two alternative modules, two F95 Mk 10 high oblique-across-track cameras for low-altitude work, or a single F126 camera for medium-altitude work. A British Aerospace (formerly Hawker Siddeley) Dynamics 401 infra-red line-scan (IRLS) is carried in the rear of the pod for increased daylight (or low-visibility) work.

Jaguar reconnaissance missions are quite similar to normal attack missions in the use of the aircraft's avionics. Turning points, IPs and targets (in this case photographic targets) are recorded in the aircraft's MCS 920M computer before take-off. The pilot simply has to turn on the camera equipment before reaching his target in order to rotate the camera drums to their pre-determined positions; then he waits for the HUD to switch to the close navigation mode two minutes from the target, at which point the target is marked for him by an acquisition marker on the HUD. Photographs are taken in a second, and it is for the pilot to decide the

French employment

After the commissioning of the first operational Armée de l'Air Jaguar squadron, EC 1/7 'Provence', the aircraft gradually eased into French service although, somewhat remarkably, the last French Jaguar was not delivered until as late as 1981. The French intention of buying 200 Jaguars, as stated in the January 1967 amendment to the original Memorandum of Understanding covering the Jaguar project, was not subsequently increased, the total French procurement comprising 40 two-seat Jaguar Es and 160 Jaguar As. All were destined for service with the Armée de l'Air following the cancellation of the Jaguar M maritime variant.

At the start of the French use of the production Jaguars, some of the initial single- and two-seat aircraft were passed to the CEAM at Mont de Marsan. The CEAM performed the pre-service trials on the aircraft before its introduction into squadron service, while a further capacity was to aid in the conversion of operational squadrons onto the Jaguar. To this end, personnel of the initial operational units were rotated through the base; this was a vitally important function, as some of these units had previously been flying aircraft which were now obsolescent and the Jaguar represented a major step forward in systems and technology. The CEAM, in collaboration with the manufacturer, also compiled technical manuals for the Armée de l'Air as well as deciding operating procedures for the Jaguar, a

similar function being carried out by the A&AEE at Boscombe Down for the RAF's aircraft.

The second French Jaguar squadron was EC 3/7 'Languedoc', which had converted to the type by December 1973. This unit, like EC 1/7, had been equipped with the Mystère IV until conversion, and was also based at St Dizier. A third squadron, EC 2/7 'Argonne', was added shortly after this, the unit being renumbered from EC 1/8, which had previously been based at Casaux. The wing's fourth squadron, EC 4/7, was added early in 1980 to bring the wing up to its full complement of four squadrons. EC 1/7, as the first operational unit, was assigned some of the earliest Jaguar As to come off the final assembly lines.

The second wing to begin converting to the Jaguar was the 11eme Escadre, based at Toul-Rosières. The principal equipment of the squadrons comprising this wing was the North American F-100 Super Sabre, which, by the mid-1970s, had come to the end of its utility as a front-line type. Conversion began during 1974, EC 3/11 'Corse' being the first to receive the Jaguar. It was operational by early 1976, and was followed by

EC 1/11 'Roussillon' and EC 2/11 'Vosges' during the remainder of 1976. EC 4/11 'Jura' was later added to the wing and, being a more recent squadron, it was assigned some of the later Jaguar As to be completed. Although the first three squadrons are based at the wing's headquarters at Toul-Rosières, EC 4/11 is home-based at Bordeaux, where it replaced the 92eme Escadre and its Sud-Ouest Vautours from 1979.

The third and last wing to be equipped with the Jaguar was the 3eme Escadre. EC 3/3 'Ardennes' was the first squadron of the wing to re-equip, this taking place during 1977. The wing's other two squadrons, EC 1/3 'Navarre' and EC 2/3 'Champagne' subsequently converted from the Mirage to the Jaguar, and the whole wing is based at Nancy.

By the time all the Jaguar squadrons had been formed, these units were grouped under the Commandement Aérien Tactique, the tactical arm of the Armée de l'Air which also had at its disposal a number of wings equipped with the Dassault Mirage IIIE ground-attack fighter. Because of the independent French military stance with regard to NATO, these units are not involved within a larger NATO military organization, and are kept entirely under national control.

Carrying a centreline drop tank and two underwing Magic air-to-air missiles, this French Jaguar A sports the fuselage code and fin insigne (a Spartan archer) of Escadre de Chasse 2/7 'Argonne'.

French Jaguars have nuclear as well as conventional strike roles. Several of the Jaguar units were assigned specific tasks, those of the 11eme Escadre being the most diverse. The role of EC 1/11, for example, was that of giving direct close support to French land forces, for which conventional weapons would be carried. EC 3/11 was deployed overseas as a part of the French armed forces' commitment to the defence of French interests and friendly countries overseas. The 3eme Escadre has a specialist wartime role of destroying hostile radar and related installations, a task performed with the Martel anti-radar missile. The 7eme Escadre has a predominantly nuclear strike role, but with EC 2/7 remaining for some time the only non-nuclear weapon carrying squadron in the wing. The main function of EC 2/7 was to carry low-level conventional weapons in support of French army units. As with their RAF counterparts, most French operational Jaguar units have a number of two-seat Jaguars assigned to them, for such duties as familiarization and unit-level training work.

The weapons provision for Armée de l'Air Jaguars is varied, and suited to the particular role expected of the various operational units flying the aircraft. The anti-radar Matra/ British Aerospace (Hawker Siddeley) Dynamics AS.37 Martel (Missile, Anti-Radar and Television) is usually carried by 3eme Escadre aircraft in keeping with their specialist anti-radar installation strike work. Various combinations of free-fall or retarded bombs can be carried, although French Jaguars are rarely seen with the common RAF ordnance of 1,000-lb (454-kg) bombs. Other air-to-ground ordnance, such as SNEB rocket pods, Matra Beluga cluster bombs (similar to the Hunting BL755 cluster bomb of the RAF Jaguars), and Matra Durandal runway-piercing bombs, can be carried. This last is a particularly effective air-to-ground weapon. When it is released

towards the target, the bomb is retarded by a parachute to increase separation from the aircraft and to provide a steep impact angle. It is then accelerated by means of a rocket engine, penetrating the runway surface and exploding below it, thus creating a large crater and area of destruction.

The Jaguar's air-to-ground strike capability will be considerably enhanced with the widespread introduction of the Aérospatiale AS.30L laser-guided air-to-surface missile. This weapon is used in conjunction with a target acquisition and designation system named ATLIS (Airborne Tracking Laser Illumination System); this equipment was developed jointly by Thomson-CSF of France and Martin Marietta of the United States. It consists of a wide-angle television camera and a laser designator mounted in a purpose-designed and -built pod carried beneath the Jaguar's fuselage on the centre weapons pylon. A television monitor

Above: The inbuilt armament of the Jaguar E (such as this EC 3/11 'Corse' aircraft) is two DEFA 553 cannon in the lower fuselage sides.

Below left: The 11th production Jaguar A is the senior aircraft of EC 3/11, the first French unit to receive the Jaguar.

Below right: EC 2/11 'Vosges' was the last of the 11ᵉ Escadre's units to receive the Jaguar, and has a specialist electronic warfare role.

EC 3/11 was the first French unit to receive the Jaguar, and now based at Toul has the non-standard complement of seven Jaguar As and eight Jaguar Es, an example of the former type being seen on a training sortie.

linked to the camera in the pod is contained within the cockpit, and is used by the pilot to pick out his target before assessing its range with the laser equipment and locking onto it with the laser designator. The missile can then be fired, after which it is guided towards the target by a laser seeker in its nose. The laser beam emitted by the ATLIS equipment remains locked onto the target until the missile hits it, even if the pilot has ceased to fly towards the general direction of the target. Attacks can be made in low-visibility conditions as well as in clear daylight, the television camera having an infra-red capability which will display the target on the cockpit-mounted television screen even if the pilot cannot visually identify the target. In the latter case, the aircraft's navigation and attack equipment

is used to bring the Jaguar to the vicinity of the target, at which point the camera can be switched on to allow the pilot to search for the target. Such a weapons-delivery system gives the French Jaguar A an important stand-off capability, which is especially necessary in cases where the target has its own strong defences which would preclude a closer free-fall attack. The final 30 French Jaguar As are fitted with ATLIS 2 equipment, the last of these being delivered to the Armée de l'Air on 14 December 1981.

The weapon which has potentially greatest destructive power amongst the French Jaguar's possible weapons is that carried by the aircraft of the 7eme Escadre. Together with a small number of Mirage III units, Jaguars of this wing can carry

the French AN-52 tactical nuclear weapon. Aircraft configured for this bomb are one branch of France's airborne nuclear forces, the other part of which is the strategic nuclear deterrent force of Dassault Mirage IV bombers.

A major step forward in providing the Jaguar with an air-to-air capability came with the installation of the French Matra R.550 Magic infra-red dog-fighting missile. The concept of using the Jaguar in an air-to-air capacity gained momentum especially with the trials leading to the Jaguar International. The aircraft had not been designed specifically to carry such weapons, but nevertheless the installation of the comparatively small Magic and Sidewinder missiles did not present many problems. Test firings of missiles positioned on both underwing

There is a great deal of systems and weapons commonality between the British and French versions of the Jaguar, and among the French-developed weapons available for the five hardpoints of the Jaguar are the AS.37 Martel anti-radar missile, the Beluga cluster bomb, the Durandal anti-runway bomb and a wide variety of Matra rocket-launcher pods.

BL755

MINISTRY OF DEFENCE

AS37 ANTI-RADAR MISSILE

and overwing pylons were made subsequently, successful live firing from the latter being made by aircraft flying from Warton during 1976; the Magic itself had made its first flight only during the early 1970s, although its potential for use by a wide range of current combat aircraft had soon been recognized. The Jaguar's overwing pylons, which are in a unique position for carrying military ordnance on a modern combat aircraft, are situated on the normally-fitted wing fence. Such a position allows the underwing pylons to be used for their normal air-to-ground ordnance. The French are fully committed to using air-to-air missiles with their Jaguars, as are export customers for the aircraft.

The transition of the Jaguar into French service was relatively smooth, although there were a number of minor problems. For

A limited stand-off capability is given to French Jaguars by the use of the BGL laser-guided bomb system developed by Matra. This comprises a laser-guidance package and flying surfaces added to standard French bombs, and ranges between 2.5 and 6.2 miles (4 and 10 km) can be achieved with the aid of a Thomson-CSF pod-mounted laser designator carried on the fuselage hardpoint.

example, various difficulties were encountered with the training of ground crews available to service the aircraft. Fortunately it was found that Jaguar maintenance was almost as straightforward as that of less complicated aircraft and it was not necessary to increase the number of specially trained ground crews. An original design consideration of the aircraft had been the maintenance factor, and a target of 10.5 MMH/FH (maintenance man-hours per flight hour) had been envisaged when the Jaguar was designed. At the time this was a particularly low figure for such a sophisticated aircraft, and compares well with the MMH/FH of many operational types, although it is interesting to note that the McDonnell Douglas F/A-18 Hornet fighter and attack aircraft, which is a comparatively recent design carrying a large amount of sophisticated equipment, itself carries a contractual guarantee of some 11 MMH/FH.

An argument raised in some quarters in France had centred on the apparently unequal avionics fit when the British and French aircraft are compared. This is especially true of the French two-seater Jaguar, which has a relatively simple equipment fit when compared to the RAF's Jaguar T.Mk 2. A major distinguishing feature between the British and French attack Jaguars is the lack of a laser designator in the nose of the French machines. Nevertheless, with the introduction of ATLIS 2 equipment in the later Jaguar As, the French have an extra capability which considerably enhances the potential of their aircraft.

With a decade of service in the Armée de l'Air behind it, the Jaguar has become well established in that air arm, and has served longer with it than with any other air force. French Jaguars have a further claim to fame, in that they have actually flown combat in a genuine shooting war. The Jaguar entered combat in December 1977 while helping to support the government of Mauritania. Problems over the future of the Spanish Sahara have created an uneasy situation in this part of north-west Africa for some years, with Polisario guerrillas demanding Saharan independence. A few Jaguars have been shot down in combat against these guerrillas, but the work carried out by the French machines has been extremely important in furthering French interests in the area and in Chad.

Export models

The export model of the Jaguar is the Jaguar International, and to date the type has been sold to Ecuador, India, Nigeria and Oman. By far the largest order has been placed by India, and the sale of the Jaguar to that country is remarkable in that it has included the provision of licence production by an indigenous Indian aircraft manufacturer.

The Jaguar International differs from the original British and French Jaguars in a number of respects, particularly in the powerplant, weapons, and the avionics installed in this variant. The Adours fitted in the export aircraft are of either the Mk 804 or the Mk 811 variety. The Mk 804 is similar to the Mk 104 retrofitted to RAF Jaguars, and has ratings of 5,320-lb (2,410-kg) dry and 8,040-lb (3,645-kg) thrust with afterburner. This gives an increase in thrust of some 27 per cent with full afterburner at Mach 0.9 at sea level over the earlier Mk 102, but the power levels attainable from the Adour

are further increased by the introduction of the Mk 811 variant. This engine has ratings of 5,520-lb (2,504-kg) thrust dry and 8,400-lb (3,811-kg) thrust with afterburner. The increase in power derived from these engines gives the Jaguar a greater flexibility in its weapon-carrying and mission profiles.

A wide range of weapons has been cleared by Warton for use with the export Jaguar, much of this follow-up work being carried out in the UK because of the greater interest shown there in the Jaguar International variant than in France, where the aircraft is direct competition in export sales with home-produced French types. Armament provision includes Magic or Sidewinder air-to-air missiles, and anti-shipping weapons such as the McDonnell Douglas AGM-84 Harpoon, Aérospatiale AM.39 Exocet, and MBB Kormoran. The anti-shipping role is again a relatively recent addition to the Jaguar's possible

missions, although it reintroduces the maritime connection which had previously been abandoned with the cancellation of the Aéronavale Jaguar M. These weapons are quite an addition to the more usual loads such as those carried by the British and French aircraft, but the increased diversity of weapons offered for the Jaguar International gives the type an added appeal to potential overseas customers.

The navigation and attack equipment carried by the export Jaguars can be suited to fit a particular customer's requirements. This has resulted in a diversity of avionics fits for overseas aircraft, and the development of systems such as low-visibility sensors and low-light-level television equipment for fitting in these aircraft as required. The multi-purpose Thomson-CSF Agave radar together with a Ferranti 105S laser ranger in the nose of the Jaguar is a particularly important variation, especially with the radar's capability in air-to-sea, air-to-ground and (particularly) air-to-air search.

The trials leading to the various equipment and engine combinations possible in the Jaguar International were well under way by the mid-1970s. One of the aircraft used in these trials was the initial Jaguar originally destined for the RAF, the first production Jaguar S-1 (XX108). Rather than entering RAF service, this aircraft had been delegated to various weapons and proving trials, and was also partnered in the Jaguar International programme by the second British single-seat prototype, Jaguar S-07 (XW563). The potential of the Jaguar for overseas sales had been

FAE302 was the second single-seat Jaguar handed over to Ecuador in 1977. The aircraft is on the strength of Escuadron de Combate 2111, part of the Ala de Combate 21 based at Taura.

The largest export customer for the Jaguar is India, whose air force has borrowed RAF aircraft pending indigenous production.

realized in the early stages of Jaguar development, and several foreign countries had been interested in the type even before the Jaguar International variant had been fully introduced.

One NATO country which showed sufficient interest to send an evaluation team to examine the aircraft at Warton in early 1974 was Belgium, which was trying to find a replacement for the Lockheed F-104G Starfighter. The West Germans were also interested at one time in buying the Jaguar. But it was not until the Farnborough air and trade show later in 1974 that the Jaguar International was officially launched. Various special sales tours and flights were duly made over the next few years, the Middle East being one particularly important market where strenuous attempts were made to obtain orders.

The greatest export success for the Jaguar to date is the substantial deal signed with India in the late 1970s for new-build and licence-manufactured Jaguars. The Indians had already established a long and successful tradition of licence building and (in some cases) further development of foreign types, which form a substantial part of the Indian Air Force (IAF) combat elements. In being chosen by the IAF in the face of large and impressive competition from various other warplanes from several countries, continued production of the Jaguar was ensured for some time to come. The IAF had realized by the start of the 1970s that it would soon be necessary to find a replace-

ment for some of the front-line types then in the Indian inventory, such as the Hunter and Canberra which by then were aging rapidly. Various possibilities were examined, including a requirement for a deep-penetration fighter-bomber specifically to replace the Canberra. Such specifications eventually attracted a variety of current Western and Soviet contenders, including the Mikoyan-Gurevich MiG-23, Sukhoi Su-20, and export variants

of the Dassault/Breguet Mirage. By this time the Jaguar was entering service with the Armée de l'Air and then the RAF, and the successful transition into service by the aircraft was an important development for the Indians as well as for other potential overseas customers, who would have been less willing to consider purchase of the aircraft if serious difficulties had arisen with the service Jaguars.

By the later 1970s, the field had narrowed to three possible

Getting the type into service with aircraft loaned by the RAF, the Indian air force plans to procure a total of 160 Jaguar Internationals.

Finished in desert camouflage, a batch of 10 Jaguar Internationals (eight single-seaters and two two-seaters) awaits delivery. The Sultan of Oman's air force currently operates 19 single-seaters and four two-seaters on Nos 8 and 20 Squadrons based at Thumrayt and Masirah respectively.

49

only occasion when the Jaguar and Mirage ended up in competition with each other for export sales; quite naturally, Dassault wished to sell its own aircraft, but the unique situation in which SEPECAT and one of its member companies were competing against each other created obvious difficulties.

After considerable evaluation by the IAF of all three main contenders, the Indian government announced on 6 October 1978 that the Jaguar had been selected to fulfil the IAF's requirements. This announcement was followed on 21 October by the signing of an Intention to Proceed (ITP) document, which would subsequently allow SEPECAT to start manufacturing the first batch of aircraft, while Hindustan Aeronautics Limited could begin preparing for the establishment of manufacturing facilities for Indian production of the Jaguar.

An important consideration in the Indian decision had been the necessity for home-production and the ease of the relevant transfer of technology. The ITP was signed by such signatories as F. W. Page for SEPECAT and Shri S. Banerji, then Defence Secretary to the Indian government. Under the terms of the contract covering the agreement, an initial batch of 40 Jaguars was to be built by SEPECAT,

Carrying the serial JI004, this Jaguar GR.Mk 1 of the Indian air force is in reality the RAF's XX117, the seventh production Jaguar S. This and other Jaguar single- and two-seaters have been lent to India so that Nos 14 and 5 Squadrons could be formed in summer 1980 and August 1981 while production of India's own Jaguars was launched (40 from BAe Warton, 45 by Hindustan Aeronautics Ltd from British-supplied components and further production by HAL from Indian manufacture).

Part of Oman's second Jaguar batch departs on its delivery flight.

contenders for the Indian deal: the Jaguar, the Swedish Saab Viggen, and the Dassault/Breguet Mirage F.1. Inclusion of the latter had turned the potential difficulty created by the previous Dassault and Breguet merger into reality; one of the member companies of SEPECAT was now attempting to sell one of its own aircraft in competition with the Jaguar. This was was not the

A Jaguar E of the 7ᵉ Escadre de Chasse shows off its leading-edge slats (which can be used in combat for additional manouevrability) and trailing-edge flaps.

with the Indians part- and wholly-manufacturing a further 120. The whole deal was worth some £1,000 million spread over a number of years, the biggest such deal ever concluded by India at that time.

The manufacture of the initial all-SEPECAT aircraft consisted of parts being supplied from France and the UK as usual, the Jaguars being put together at Warton before flying out to India. The first 40 aircraft were to comprise 35 strike Jaguars and five two-seat trainers. Delivery began in February 1981 of the first of these aircraft, although by this time the Jaguar had already entered Indian service. The first machines supplied to India were originally RAF Jaguars, which were handed over to the IAF to allow indoctrination on the type and the formation of initial squadrons equipped with the Jaguar. To this end, 18 ex-RAF single- and two-seat Jaguars were handed over to the Indians on loan, the first two on 19 July 1979, when a single- and a two-seat aircraft were delivered to the Indians at Warton before flying out to India. The first IAF Jaguar squadron, No. 14, was sub-

Part of India's 40-aircraft order for Jaguar Internationals awaits delivery from the BAe factory at Warton, home of British Jaguar production. These aircraft have Adour Mk 804 afterburning turbofans.

sequently declared operational by the summer of 1980, while the second, No. 5 Squadron, gained operational status in the summer of 1981.

A production line for the manufacture of Indian Jaguars is run by Hindustan Aeronautics at Bangalore, and the first aircraft constructed at this facility was made from parts supplied from Warton. The first components left for India on 5 May 1981 and the first Bangalore-assembled aircraft made its first flight on 31 March 1982. A total of 45 Jaguars was planned for production in this way, after which full manufacture of the whole aircraft would switch to the Indian factory. The exact number of Jaguars to be built wholly in India has been subject to various amendments, although the IAF eventually intends to receive over 100 Jaguars.

IAF Jaguars have new navigation and attacks avionics, which include a French Sagem Uliss 82 inertial navigation system, a Smiths Industries dual-mode HUD, a weapons-aiming system similar to that in the BAe Sea Harrier, and a Ferranti COMED 2045 combined map and electronic display. The initial batch of 40 Jaguars supplied to India were to be fitted with the Adour Mk 804, but all subsequent aircraft have the Adour Mk 811 installed. In addition to ordinary strike squadrons, India had a requirement for a squadron of Jaguars configured in the anti-shipping role with the Agave nose radar, a task which received much attention at Warton. Trials with Indian-designed launchers for overwing dogfighting Magic missiles have been pursued in India, the Indian Jaguars being able to carry these weapons in addition to their normal strike weapons.

Next to the substantial Indian deal, the largest number of export Jaguars has been supplied to Oman. This country was, with

Ecuador, the first purchaser of the Jaguar International, both countries ordering the aircraft in 1974. The Omani order, awarded in August 1974, covered 12 Jaguars, of which all but two would be of the single-seat strike variant. This batch of Jaguars was part of the then current Omani attempts to improve the country's air-defence system, other contracts being awarded at the same time for the supply of British Aerospace Dynamics Rapier surface-to-air missiles, and ground radar and communications equipment. Initial deliveries were subsequently made from 7 March 1977, when the Sultan of Oman's Air Force (SOAF) received one single-seat and one two-seat Jaguar. The Jaguars duly went on to equip No. 8 Squadron at Thumrayt, being used in strike and air-defence duties. Until this time, parts of Oman's air defences had been made up of Imperial Iranian Air Force aircraft, but the appearance of the Jaguar allowed Oman to fulfil this role itself. All the 12 Jaguars had been delivered by the spring of 1978. A re-order for an additional 12 Jaguars was received in the middle of 1980, again as part of a deal covering other defence equipment, in this case an order for improved Rapier radar systems and related equipment. A second squadron was formed to operate these Jaguars and construction of the aircraft was completed in 1983.

The first 12 SOAF Jaguars were fitted with Adour Mk 804s, but the second batch received the improved Adour Mk 811 engine. Omani Jaguars are configured to carry air-to-air missiles in keeping with their air-defence role, the aircraft in the initial batch being fitted with overwing launch rails for Magic missiles, while the later aircraft have the outboard underwing pylons adapted to carry AIM

(Air Intercept Missile)-9P Sidewinders. All SOAF Jaguars carry a Marconi 920ATC NAVWASS computer, a unit with double the capability and twice the power of the MCS 920M computer fitted to the RAF machines.

The order from Ecuador announced during 1974 covered the supply of 12 aircraft, and these were the first export Jaguars to be supplied. The first Jaguar of this order, which carried the 'B' Condition serial number G-27-266 before delivery, initially flew on 19 August 1976 as the first Jaguar International to fly. Ten of the Jaguars were single-seaters, while the other two (including G-27-266) were two-seaters. Deliveries began in January 1977, being completed by October of that year; the aircraft were flown, rather than shipped, to Ecuador and their navigation equipment was extremely useful for this large undertaking. Like the Omani Jaguars, the Ecuadorian aircraft operate in extreme conditions which had not been fully envisaged when the type was first designed. Nevertheless, the Jaguar has shown itself fully capable of operating in the hot and humid climates in which it flies, as well as on the high-altitude airfields found in Ecuador, an important extra selling point for any future prospective customers.

The most recent export success for the Jaguar was an order for 18 aircraft to be supplied to Nigeria. By the end of 1983 several of these Jaguars had been completed but not delivered. The military coup which ended civilian rule in Nigeria at the end of December 1983 created some questions over the future of the Jaguar in Nigerian military service because the aircraft had been ordered by the overthrown civilian administration.

Experimental versions

One of the most important current research projects being undertaken with a view to producing future advanced combat aircraft is centred almost entirely on the test flying of a single experimental Jaguar in the UK. This aircraft is XX765, originally one of the 165 Jaguar GR.Mk 1s destined for RAF service, but subsequently directed to become a flying test-bed for Active Control Technology (ACT) systems. The aircraft is considerably altered from the standard Jaguar GR.Mk 1, and is not intended as the basis of a future mark of Jaguar. It is a one-off research aircraft to test the systems to be included in future combat aircraft.

Installed in this FBW Jaguar is an advanced all-digital quadruplex fly-by-wire (FBW) control system, which requires no form of emergency back-up equipment, and contains systems constructed to production standard. This type of equipment was flown for the first time anywhere in the world when

XX765 took to the air on its first flight after conversion on 20 October 1981. The aircraft was flown by Chris Yeo, Senior Experimental Test Pilot at BAe Warton where the aircraft is usually based. The test project had been initiated in 1977 by the Ministry of Defence (MOD), after successful results were achieved in studies carried out by BAe's Warton and related facilities. The MOD has subsequently funded the whole programme and given active support to it. Major subcontractors in the project are the Combat Aircraft Controls Division of Marconi Avionics Limited (which provides the avionics and high-speed digital computers which are the heart of the control systems), and Dowty Boulton Paul Limited (which provides the servo actuator controls for spoilers, rudder, and tailplane).

The fly-by-wire controls system basically replaces the Jaguar's normal controls, such as the mechanical units and control rods, used to operate the con-

ventional control surfaces on the wings and tail of the aircraft. In their place are fitted four independent electrical channels which relay instructions to the control surfaces by means of electronic impulses issued by four high-speed, mutually self-monitoring computers. These are linked to two subsidiary actuator drive and monitor computers and other failure-compensating equipment, with the result that the whole system can automatically survive all probable failures in the system, and hence no emergency back-up is necessary. Instructions for the control surfaces are provided through this electronic system not only on the instructions of the pilot as he flies the aircraft, but are also given automatically to correct any uncommanded motions detected by sensors mounted in the aircraft. Response to all commands is instantaneous, and the computers are programmed to ensure that they only issue commands which are

Designed to validate British active-control technology, the FBW Jaguar is a Jaguar GR.Mk 1 modified with digital quadruplex fly-by-wire controls without manual reversion.

The FBW Jaguar includes Marconi avionics (with high-speed digital computers) and Dowty Boulton Paul electronically-controlled servo actuators.

within the limits of the airframe's capabilities.

The system saves a great deal of weight, in doing away with the normal hardware associated with the mechanical operation of an aircraft's control surfaces, but its great advantage is that it allows an unstable aircraft to fly. This is vital for future combat aircraft designs. It allows the aircraft to fly with far more agility and manoeuvrability than a conventionally controlled aircraft, and a smaller, lighter, and more agile fighter aircraft will be a future product of the successful FBW Jaguar trials; indeed, the BAe Agile Combat Aircraft is one future design which will benefit from the test programme. With the new control system, the future fighter will be freely manoeuvred by the pilot to suit the particular combat situation at any given moment, while not asking him to make many of the demanding number of control and flying decisions associated with this type of flying.

XX765's trial programme has subsequently included flights in an unstable configuration. This is created by the installation of ballast in the rear fuselage and of leading-edge root extensions along the upper edges of the inlet trunks. The aircraft is then bombarded with simulated lightning strikes to check the working of the ACT systems under this kind of atmospheric condition. All the trials undertaken with this aircraft have been a great success, proving that the advanced control system has a practical application which means that it could be installed in many selected combat aircraft with relative ease.

One of the most important recent projects associated with possible future development of the Jaguar itself concerns the creation of an improved aircraft with yet more powerful Adour engines. Various ideas to this effect have existed for some time, but the concept of turning them into a viable project came to fruition in the late 1970s. The plan for a Super Jaguar was revealed in some detail at the 1979 Paris air and trade show. Some of the features discussed at this time have now been included; for example, one of the important systems which was to be incorporated in the aircraft was the Agave radar which is now an important option for the Jaguar International.

The Super Jaguar was to retain the standard Jaguar's considerable strike ability, but the intention was to extend it and also give the aircraft a viable air-to-air capability. This was where the installation of the Agave radar proved fruitful, although even more powerful Adours than the Mk 811 of the Jaguar International were envisaged, in order to give the design a considerable performance ability when combating aircraft designed as fighters from the outset. The most important feature of the Super Jaguar was to have been its wing, however. A completely new wing was envisaged, either built completely out of metal or constructed from carbonfibre and other composite materials. The use of carbonfibre in the Jaguar's airframe has been discussed on a number of occasions, but in this case the material was to have been of primary importance. The new wing was envisaged as being of completely new design, with a comparatively larger area; this allowed for an increase in fuel capacity, and the introduction of six new weapons pylons under the wings. A drooping leading edge and flaperons were introduced to give better dog-fighting agility.

Experimental projects tend to disappear unless sufficient interest or backing can be found, and in the 1960s a Jaguar derivative was dropped for this reason. This was to have been a single-engine variable-geometry ('swing-wing') design, bearing a superficial resemblance to the Jaguar itself and constructed as a joint project between the UK and Australia. The British government did not provide the necessary interest or backing and the project disappeared. It seems unlikely at present that the Super Jaguar will appear either, although the interest in carbon-fibre technology was sufficient to result in development contracts being placed for a carbonfibre wing.

The future

First conceived as a viable project during the 1960s, the Jaguar has given valuable years of service and seems set to be a front-line type for many years to come, particularly with the emergence of important export sales and continuing production of the aircraft. Both the Armée de l'Air and the RAF envisage the Jaguar as remaining in service for some years, and indeed the former has an up-dating programme which will keep its aircraft in service at least until the end of the 1980s.

Within the RAF, the established Jaguar force will be gradually altered as more Tornado GR.Mk 1s come into service. This development will change the appearance of RAF Germany in particular, where the Tornado will eventually replace all the Jaguar squadrons. The main limitation with the Jaguar's otherwise excellent avionics fit is that it does not have a full all-weather/ day and night capability, a capability now considered vital, especially in the context of possible European combat operations. The Tornado, contain- ing a comprehensive all-weather avionics fit and a second crew member to work its systems, has this capability and is already well established within the RAF. The question of a Jaguar replacement has already been under discussion for some time, not because of any shortcomings in the aircraft but because, with the time now taken in the creation of modern warplanes, future requirements have to be examined well in advance. The Jaguar requirement was embodied in AST.403, and it is certain that the design which is eventually to develop as the Jaguar's replace- ment will have to be a formidable aircraft indeed in order to live up to the Jaguar's great advance in capability and to the tradition of reliable service which the air- craft has established for itself within some of the most important air forces in the West.

The FBW Jaguar takes off on its maiden flight on 20 October 1981. By 1984 the aircraft had been fitted with large leading-edge strakes to become a true control-configured vehicle.

Jaguar GR.Mk 1

Type: single-seat tactical strike and ground-attack fighter

Accommodation: pilot only, seated on a Martin-Baker 9B Mk II zero/zero ejector seat

Armament: two 30-mm Aden cannon with ? rounds per gun, plus five external hardpoints for a total load of 10,000 lb (4,536 kg) including a tactical nuclear weapon, bombs, rocket pods, air-to-surface missiles and other weapons

Powerplant: two Rolls-Royce/Turboméca Adour Mk 104 turbofans, each rated at 5,320-lb (2,413-kg) dry thrust and 8,040-lb (3,647-kg) afterburning thrust

Performance:
maximum speed 1,056 mph (1,699 km/h) or Mach 1.6 at altitude
cruising speed —
initial climb rate 30,000 ft (9,145 m) in 1 minute 30 seconds
service ceiling 45,930 ft (14,000 m)
range 334-mile (537-km) lo-lo-lo tactical radius on internal fuel, or 875-mile (1,408-km) hi-lo-hi tactical radius with external fuel, and 2,190-mile (3,524-km) ferry range with external fuel

Weights:
empty equipped 15,432 lb (7,000 kg)
normal take-off 24,149 lb (10,954 kg)
maximum take-off 34,612 lb (15,700 kg)

Dimensions:
span 28 ft 6 in (8.69 m)
length 55 ft 2½ in (16.83 m) with probe and 50 ft 11 in (15.52 m) without probe
height 16 ft 0½ in (4.89 m)
wing area 260.27 sq ft (24.18 m²)

Jaguar A

Type: single-seat tactical strike and ground-attack fighter

Accommodation: pilot only, seated on a Martin-Baker JRM4 ejector seat

Armament: two 30-mm DEFA cannon with ? rounds per gun, plus five external hardpoints for a total load of 10,000 lb (4,536 kg) including a tactical nuclear weapon, bombs, rocket pods, air-to-surface missiles and other weapons

Powerplant: two Rolls-Royce/Turboméca Adour Mk 102 turbofans, each rated at 5,115-lb (2,320-kg) dry thrust and 7,305-lb (3,314-kg) afterburning thrust

Performance:
maximum speed 1,056 mph (1,699 km/h) or Mach 1.6 at altitude
cruising speed —
initial climb rate slightly inferior to that of Jaguar GR.Mk 1
service ceiling 45,930 ft (14,000 m)
range comparable with that of Jaguar GR.Mk 1

Weights:
empty equipped 15,432 lb (7,000 kg)
normal take-off 24,149 lb (10,954 kg)
maximum take-off 34,612 lb (15,700 kg)

Dimensions:
span 28 ft 6 in (8.69 m)
length 55 ft 2½ in (16.83 m) with probe and 50 ft 11 in (15.52 m) without probe
height 16 ft 0½ in (4.89 m)
wing area 260.27 sq ft (24.18 m²)

Jaguar International

Type: single-seat tactical support aircraft

Accommodation: pilot only, seated on a Martin-Baker E9B (Ecuador), O9B (Oman), IN9B (India) or N9B (Nigeria) zero/zero ejector seat

Armament: two 30-mm DEFA or Aden cannon with ? rounds per gun, plus seven external hardpoints for a total load of up to 10,500 lb (4.763 kg): 10,000 lb (4,536 kg) of this comprises non-nuclear stores of the type carried by the Jaguar A and S, and 500 lb (227 kg) is allowed for two AIM-9 Sidewinder or Matra Magic air-to-air missiles carried on overwing hardpoints

Powerplant: two Rolls-Royce/Turboméca Adour Mk 811 turbofans, each rated at 5,520-lb (2,504-kg) dry thrust and 9,270-lb (4,205-kg) afterburning thrust

Performance:
maximum speed 1,056 mph (1,699 km/h) or Mach 1.6 at altitude
cruising speed —
initial climb rate 30,000 ft (9,145 m) in 1 minute 30 seconds
service ceiling 45,930 ft (14,000 m)
range 332-mile (535-km) tactical radius on a lo-lo-lo mission

Weights:
empty equipped 16,975 lb (7,700 kg)
normal take-off —
maximum take-off 34,612 lb (15,700 kg)

Dimensions:
span 28 ft 6 in (8.69 m)
length —
height 16 ft 0½ in (4.89 m)
wing area 260.27 sq ft (24.18 m²)

Jaguar T.Mk 2

Type: two-seat operational conversion trainer with secondary strike and ground-attack capability

Accommodation: pilot and instructor, seated in tandem on Martin-Baker 9B Mk II ejector seats

Armament: one 30-mm Aden cannon with ? rounds, plus five external hardpoints for a total load of 10,000 lb (4,536 kg) including a tactical nuclear weapon, bombs, rocket pods, air-to-surface missiles and other weapons

Powerplant: two Rolls-Royce (Turboméca Adour Mk 104 turbofans, each rated at 5,320-lb (2,413-kg) dry thrust and 8,040-lb (3,647-kg) afterburning thrust

Performance:
maximum speed 1,056 mph (1,699 km/h) or Mach 1.6 at altitude
cruising speed —
initial climb rate 30,000 ft (9,145 m) in 1 minute 30 seconds
service ceiling 45,930 ft (14,000 m)
range comparable with that of Jaguar GR.Mk 1

Weights:
empty equipped 15,432 lb (7,000 kg)
normal take-off —
maximum take-off 34,612 lb (15,700 kg)

Dimensions:
span 28 ft 6 in (8.69 m)
length 57 ft 6¼ in (17.53 m) with probe and 53 ft 10½ in (16.42 m) without probe
height 16 ft 0½ in (4.89 m)
wing area 260.27 sq ft (24.18 m²)

Jaguar E

Type: two-seat advanced and operational conversion trainer with secondary tactical strike and ground-attack capability

Accommodation: pilot and instructor, seated in tandem on Martin-Baker JRM4 ejector seats

Armament: two 30-mm DEFA cannon with ? rounds per gun, plus five external hardpoints for a total load of up to 10,000 lb (4,536 kg) including a tactical nuclear weapon, bombs, rocket pods, air-to-surface and other weapons

Powerplant: two Rolls-Royce/Turboméca Adour Mk 102 turbofans, each rated at 5,115-lb (2,320-kg) dry thrust and 7,305-lb (3,314-kg) afterburning thrust

Performance:
maximum speed 1,056 mph (1,699 km/h) or Mach 1.6 at altitude
cruising speed —
initial climb rate comparable with that of Jaguar A
service ceiling 45,930 ft (14,000 m)
range comparable with that of Jaguar A

Weights:
empty equipped 15,432 lb (7,000 kg)
normal take-off —
maximum take-off 34,612 lb (15,700 kg)

Dimensions:
span 28 ft 6 in (8.69 m)
length 57 ft 6¼ in (17.53 m) with probe and 53 ft 10½ in (16.42 m) without probe
height 16 ft 0½ in (4.89 m)
wing area 260.27 sq ft (24.18 m²)

Acknowledgments

We would particularly like to thank Mr Geoffrey Hill of British Aerospace Aircraft Group, Warton for his invaluable help with illustrations for this publication.

Picture research was through Military Archive & Research Services, Braceborough, Lincolnshire and unless otherwise indicated below all material was supplied by British Aerospace.

Aerospatiale: 20.
Austin Brown: 24 (centre).
Crown Copyright (MOD-RAF): Front cover, 4, 16 (bottom), 21, 28 (top), 30, 31, 33 (bottom), 36.
Engins Matra: 43 (top), 44 (top).
Flight International: 6–7.
Martin-Baker Engineering: 26.
SIRPA (Air): 8–9, 27, 39, 40, 41, 42, 45, 51 (top).
RAF Germany: 2–3, 22 (top).
Rolls-Royce Ltd: 16 (top), 19 (bottom), 22 (bottom), 37.
Smiths Industries Ltd: 19 (top), 25.